The Essential Buyer's Guide

MERCEDES-BENZ

S-CLASS

W116-series 1972 to 1980

Your marque expert:
Julian Parish

VELOCE PUBLISHING
THE PUBLISHER OF FINE AUTOMOTIVE BOOKS

Alfa Romeo Alfasud (Metcalfe)
Alfa Romeo Alfetta: all saloon/sedan models 1972 to 1984 & coupé models 1974 to 1987 (Metcalfe)
Alfa Romeo Giulia GT Coupé (Booker)
Alfa Romeo Giulia Spider (Booker)
Audi TT (Davies)
Audi TT Mk2 2006 to 2014 (Durnan)
Austin-Healey Big Healeys (Trummel)
BMW Boxer Twins (Henshaw)
BMW E30 3 Series 1981 to 1994 (Hosier)
BMW GS (Henshaw)
BMW X5 (Saunders)
BMW Z3 Roadster (Fishwick)
BMW Z4: E85 Roadster and E86 Coupé including M and Alpina 2003 to 2009 (Smitheram)
BSA 350, 441 & 500 Singles (Henshaw)
BSA 500 & 650 Twins (Henshaw)
BSA Bantam (Henshaw)
Choosing, Using & Maintaining Your Electric Bicycle (Henshaw)
Citroën 2CV (Paxton)
Citroën DS & ID (Heilig)
Cobra Replicas (Ayre)
Corvette C2 Sting Ray 1963-1967 (Falconer)
Datsun 240Z 1969 to 1973 (Newlyn)
DeLorean DMC-12 1981 to 1983 (Williams)
Ducati Bevel Twins (Falloon)
Ducati Desmodue Twins (Falloon)
Ducati Desmoquattro Twins – 851, 888, 916, 996, 998, ST4 1988 to 2004 (Falloon)
Fiat 500 & 600 (Bobbitt)
Ford Capri (Paxton)
Ford Escort Mk1 & Mk2 (Williamson)
Ford Focus RS/ST 1st Generation (Williamson)
Ford Model A – All Models 1927 to 1931 (Buckley)
Ford Model T – All models 1909 to 1927 (Barker)
Ford Mustang – First Generation 1964 to 1973 (Cook)
Ford Mustang – Fifth Generation (2005-2014) (Cook)
Ford RS Cosworth Sierra & Escort (Williamson)
Harley-Davidson Big Twins (Henshaw)
Hillman Imp (Morgan)
Hinckley Triumph triples & fours 750, 900, 955, 1000, 1050, 1200 – 1991-2009 (Henshaw)
Honda CBR FireBlade (Henshaw)
Honda CBR600 Hurricane (Henshaw)
Honda SOHC Fours 1969-1984 (Henshaw)
Jaguar E-Type 3.8 & 4.2 litre (Crespin)
Jaguar E-type V12 5.3 litre (Crespin)
Jaguar Mark 1 & 2 (All models including Daimler 2.5-litre V8) 1955 to 1969 (Thorley)
Jaguar New XK 2005-2014 (Thorley)
Jaguar S-Type – 1999 to 2007 (Thorley)
Jaguar X-Type – 2001 to 2009 (Thorley)
Jaguar XJ-S (Crespin)
Jaguar XJ6, XJ8 & XJR (Thorley)
Jaguar XK 120, 140 & 150 (Thorley)
Jaguar XK8 & XKR (1996-2005) (Thorley)
Jaguar/Daimler XJ 1994-2003 (Crespin)
Jaguar/Daimler XJ40 (Crespin)
Jaguar/Daimler XJ6, XJ12 & Sovereign (Crespin)
Kawasaki Z1 & Z900 (Orritt)
Land Rover Discovery Series 1 (1989-1998) (Taylor)
Land Rover Discovery Series 2 (1998-2004) (Taylor)
Land Rover Series I, II & IIA (Thurman)
Land Rover Series III (Thurman)
Lotus Elan, S1 to Sprint and Plus 2 to Plus 2S 130/5 1962 to 1974 (Vale)
Lotus Europa, S1, S2, Twin-cam & Special 1966 to 1975 (Vale)
Lotus Seven replicas & Caterham 7: 1973-2013 (Hawkins)
Mazda MX-5 Miata (Mk1 1989-97 & Mk2 98-2001) (Crook)
Mazda RX-8 (Parish)
Mercedes-Benz 190: all 190 models (W201 series) 1982 to 1993 (Parish)

Mercedes-Benz 280-560SL & SLC (Bass)
Mercedes-Benz G-Wagen (Greene)
Mercedes-Benz Pagoda 230SL, 250SL & 280SL roadsters & coupés (Bass)
Mercedes-Benz S-Class W126 Series (Zoporowski)
Mercedes-Benz S-Class Second Generation W116 Series (Parish)
Mercedes-Benz SL R129-series 1989 to 2001 (Parish)
Mercedes-Benz SLK (Bass)
Mercedes-Benz W123 (Parish)
Mercedes-Benz W124 – All models 1984-1997 (Zoporowski)
MG Midget & A-H Sprite (Horler)
MG TD, TF & TF1500 (Jones)
MGA 1955-1962 (Crosier)
MGB & MGB GT (Williams)
MGF & MG TF (Hawkins)
Mini (Paxton)
Morris Minor & 1000 (Newell)
Moto Guzzi 2-valve big twins (Falloon)
New Mini (Collins)
Norton Commando (Henshaw)
Peugeot 205 GTI (Blackburn)
Piaggio Scooters – all modern two-stroke & four-stroke automatic models 1991 to 2016 (Willis)
Porsche 356 (Johnson)
Porsche 911 (964) (Streather)
Porsche 911 (993) (Streather)
Porsche 911 (996) (Streather)
Porsche 911 (997) – Model years 2004 to 2009 (Streather)
Porsche 911 (997) – Second generation models 2009 to 2012 (Streather)
Porsche 911 Carrera 3.2 (Streather)
Porsche 911SC (Streather)
Porsche 924 – All models 1976 to 1988 (Hodgkins)
Porsche 928 (Hemmings)
Porsche 930 Turbo & 911 (930) Turbo (Streather)
Porsche 944 (Higgins)
Porsche 981 Boxster & Cayman (Streather)
Porsche 986 Boxster (Streather)
Porsche 987 Boxster and Cayman 1st generation (2005-2009) (Streather)
Porsche 987 Boxster and Cayman 2nd generation (2009-2012) (Streather)
Range Rover – First Generation models 1970 to 1996 (Taylor)
Range Rover – Second Generation 1994-2001 (Taylor)
Range Rover – Third Generation L322 (2002-2012) (Taylor)
Rolls-Royce Silver Shadow & Bentley T-Series (Bobbitt)
Rover 2000, 2200 & 3500 (Marrocco)
Royal Enfield Bullet (Henshaw)
Subaru Impreza (Hobbs)
Sunbeam Alpine (Barker)
Triumph 350 & 500 Twins (Henshaw)
Triumph Bonneville (Henshaw)
Triumph Herald & Vitesse (Ayre)
Triumph Spitfire and GT6 (Ayre)
Triumph Stag (Mort)
Triumph Thunderbird, Trophy & Tiger (Henshaw)
Triumph TR2 & TR3 - All models (including 3A & 3B) 1953 to 1962 (Conners)
Triumph TR4/4A & TR5/250 - All models 1961 to 1968 (Child & Battyll)
Triumph TR6 (Williams)
Triumph TR7 & TR8 (Williams)
Triumph Trident & BSA Rocket III (Rooke)
TVR Chimaera and Griffith (Kitchen)
TVR S-series (Kitchen)
Velocette 350 & 500 Singles 1946 to 1970 (Henshaw)
Vespa Scooters – Classic 2-stroke models 1960-2008 (Paxton)
Volkswagen Bus (Copping)
Volkswagen Transporter T4 (1990-2003) (Copping/Cservenka)
VW Golf GTI (Copping)
VW Beetle (Copping)
Volvo 700/900 Series (Beavis)
Volvo P1800/1800S, E & ES 1961 to 1973 (Murray)

www.veloce.co.uk

First published January 2020 by Veloce Publishing Limited, Veloce House, Parkway Farm Business Park, Middle Farm Way, Poundbury, Dorchester DT1 3AR, England. Fax 01305 268864 / e-mail info@veloce.co.uk / web www.veloce.co.uk or www.velocebooks.com.
ISBN 978-1-787115-63-7 / UPC 6-36847-01563-3

Introduction
– the purpose of this book

The first Mercedes-Benz model to be officially called the S-Class (for Sonderklasse or 'Special' Class), the W116 Series set new standards in performance, comfort and safety when it was launched in 1972. Designed by Friedrich Geiger, the new body had a formal, imposing appearance, with Mercedes' trademark vertical headlamps of the 1960s replaced by horizontal units. Like every S-Class since, it was a symbol of success. Remarkably for such an expensive luxury model, the 450 SEL was named European Car of the Year in 1973.

The W116 offered a choice of smooth six- and eight-cylinder petrol engines, culminating in the hugely powerful 450 SEL 6.9, as well as a more economical turbodiesel for the North American market. Only available from the factory as a saloon (sedan) – in standard and long-wheelbase versions – nearly half a million cars were built at Sindelfingen during its eight-year career.

Mercedes was one of the few manufacturers at the time to have its own wind tunnel, and the W116 was much more efficient aerodynamically than its predecessors. It was technically advanced, too, with a new design of semi-trailing arm rear suspension and anti-dive and anti-squat geometry. Over time, many of the features introduced on the S-Class would work their way down Mercedes' range.

The 450 SEL 6.9 was an exceptional car: engineered to the highest standards, and, fitted with a sophisticated hydropneumatic suspension, it was a more civilised successor to the 300 SEL 6.3. Used by many F1 drivers in the day –

A green W116 flanked by its predecessors and the W126, which succeeded it.
(Courtesy Mercedes-Benz Classic)

including James Hunt and Niki Lauda – it produced 286bhp and torque of 405lb/ft in European trim, delivering tremendous performance. When new, it was more expensive in the UK than the Rolls-Royce Silver Shadow.

Today, the W116 is emerging from the shadows as a sought-after model with classic looks but which still feels modern to drive. Very much a car of the 1970s, its body has large bumpers and an abundance of chrome trim, while inside you will find luxurious velour upholstery on many models. The 6.9 already commands high prices, but the other versions can still be found for a more modest outlay.

Regardless of specification, however, many cars were originally used hard,

Alloy wheels and chrome trim set off this concours standard 450 SEL 6.9.

and there are few left in good original condition with a clear history. Repairs and restoration work can be costly and may have been poorly executed. If well looked after, however, these cars can easily cover high mileages. This guide should help you find the right car at a fair price.

Thanks

This guide would not have been possible without the help of several marque specialists: Edward Hall, Jonathan Aucott of Avantgarde Classics and Hervé Chauvin at GGE Classic. Rachel Goodwin and Silvie Kiefer at Mercedes-Benz provided me with access to information and archive images. I would also like to thank Alexandre Puigvert, Alan Brooks, Iris Hummel at Artcurial Motorcars, Dirk de Jager and Christophe Gasco, as well as Lynnie Farrant and Marcus Howard-Vyse at Bonhams for their help in supplying photographs. Finally, my thanks are due, as ever, to Rod Grainger and the team at Veloce Publishing.

Contents

The Essential Buyer's Guide™ currency
At the time of publication a BG unit of currency "●" equals approximately
£1.00/US$1.32/Euro1.18. Please adjust to suit current exchange rates
using Sterling as the base currency.

1 Is it the right car for you?

– marriage guidance

Tall and short drivers

All drivers should find plenty of room to get comfortable behind the wheel.

Weight of controls

The major controls are very manageable, as all W116 S-Class models were fitted with power steering and servo-assisted disc brakes all round, and the majority of cars were equipped with automatic transmission.

Will it fit in the garage?

Model	Length	Width	Height
Standard-wheelbase (European bumpers)	195.3in/4960mm	73.4-73.6in/ 1865-1870mm	56.1-56.3in/ 1425-1430mm
Long-wheelbase (European bumpers)	199.2in/5060mm	73.4-73.6in/ 1865-1870mm	56.1-56.3in/ 1425-1430mm
300 SD (US-spec safety bumpers)	205.5in/5220mm	73.6in/1870mm	56.1in/1425mm

Interior space

The W116 was a large car for its time, and there is generous space for four or

Luxurious rear seats in a long-wheelbase 450 SEL.
(Courtesy Artcurial Motorcars/Dirk de Jager)

even five passengers. Standard versions offer only average rear legroom, but the L models have a 10cm (4in) longer wheelbase, allowing those in the back to stretch out in comfort.

Luggage capacity
The W116 has a spacious boot (trunk) with a capacity of 18.7ft^3 (530l). It has a relatively high load lip, however, and the rear seat backrest does not fold down.

Usability
Like so many classic Mercedes, the W116 is a practical and durable car. The interior is ergonomically designed and some cars have modern equipment such as air-conditioning and cruise control. The 450 SEL 6.9's combination of performance, ride and handling remains the equal of many more recent sports saloons. It is probably only the relatively high fuel consumption of all models and the wish to preserve their cars which dissuades many owners from using them more often.

Parts availability
In general, parts supply is worse than for Mercedes' W123 and W124 models, with fewer cars left to strip for spares. Some mechanical parts were shared with the R107 SL roadsters, introduced a year before the W116. Mercedes-Benz itself can still supply many mechanical components, but body panels and windscreens, electrical items such as headlights, chrome and other trim can be harder to source. This is especially the case for interior parts in less common materials and colours such as moss green velour. Mercedes occasionally re-manufactures batches of

Chrome trim can be difficult or expensive to replace.
(Courtesy Artcurial Motorcars/Dirk de Jager)

parts when demand builds up, while there are a number of independent specialists, particularly in Germany, who can often come to the rescue.

Service costs
The recommended service interval for the W116 when new was 5000 miles (8000km), which is more than most owners will now cover in a year, and most consumables are readily available and reasonably priced. The 6.9 had many unique mechanical components and is significantly more expensive to maintain.

Insurance
All W116s are now at least 40 years old and should be eligible for classic car policies, sometimes with mileage restrictions or alongside a newer everyday car.

Investment potential
As it is rediscovered by collectors, values of all versions of the W116 are likely to increase. As a rule, however, it is Mercedes' sports cars and top-of-the-range models that have offered the best return on investment; the 6.9 already commands a significant premium over the rest of the range and this looks likely to continue.

450 SEL 6.9 is the best choice as an investment. (Courtesy Bonhams)

Foibles
The W116 is the epitome of rational design. Only the foot-operated parking brake on left-hand drive cars may take some getting used to.

Plus points
- Classic styling, but modern to drive
- Excellent ride and handling
- Superb build quality and finish

Minus points
* 6.9 excepted, not particularly sporting
* Relatively heavy fuel consumption
* Only available as a four-door saloon

Alternatives
BMW 7-Series (E23), Cadillac Seville, Jaguar XJ6/XJ12, Rolls-Royce Silver Shadow.

Jaguar's XJ6 and XJ12 models had a different, British take on luxury motoring, and were much more affordable.

2 Cost considerations
– affordable, or a money pit?

Purchase price

Prices for all models are generally lower in the UK and the US than in continental Europe, especially in Germany. Six-cylinder cars in excellent (but not concours) condition may be found in the range of ●x9,000-12,000, while the best 350 and 450 V8-engined models (especially the 450 SEL) can reach ●x15,000 plus. In the US, 300 SD models will be slightly cheaper. The 450 SEL 6.9 is in a different league: reckon on paying at least twice the price of a standard 450 SEL, with the best examples reaching ●x50-60,000.

Running costs

Routine service parts for the W116 are widely available and most prices are reasonable, at least for a large, prestige saloon. The exception is for parts specific to the 450 SEL 6.9, such as the hydropneumatic suspension components or the original Michelin tyres. Body and trim parts for all versions are frequently much more expensive and sometimes hard to locate.

Fuel consumption may not be a major consideration if your planned annual mileage is low, but none of the petrol-engined W116 models are particularly economical. Even the 280 models will do 20mpg (Imp)/16mpg (US) or less, and you may see as little as 12mpg (Imp)/10mpg (US) from the 6.9.

Parts prices

Prices shown are for a 450 SEL, with some parts specific to the 6.9 also shown.

Crowded engine compartment on 450 SEL 6.9. (Courtesy GGE Classic)

They are based on OEM parts from Mercedes-Benz when these are still available, or from reputable independent suppliers if not. Few cars are being scrapped nowadays, so this is rarely a reliable source of supply.

Mechanical parts
Fuel filter ⬤x50
Fuel pump ⬤x360
Sparkplugs (set of eight) ⬤x25
Timing chain kit ⬤x135
Water pump ⬤x390
Front shock absorber (each) ⬤x190
Rear shock absorber (each) ⬤x165
Steering damper ⬤x35
Front brake pads (pair) ⬤x35
Front brake discs/rotors (pair) ⬤x270
Rear brake pads (pair) ⬤x35
Rear brake discs/rotors (pair) ⬤x80
Tyre: 205/70 VR 14 (Michelin XWX)
⬤x275 (independent)
Battery ⬤x150

Suspension sphere visible under front wheelarch of 450 SEL 6.9.

For 450 SEL 6.9
Hydropneumatic suspension height control valve ⬤x1440 (independent)
Hydropneumatic suspension pump (rebuilt) ⬤x750 (independent)
Tyre: 215/70 VR 14 (Michelin XWX) ⬤x465 (independent)

Body parts
Bonnet ⬤x600 (independent)
Under bonnet insulation ⬤x40 (independent)
Radiator grille (cowling only) ⬤x640 (independent)

Traditional painted hubcaps still fitted as standard.

Rear wing ●x660 (independent)
Front door ●x600 (independent)
Door seals (set of four) ●x300 (independent)
Boot lid ●x1070 (independent)
Windscreen ●x445
Hubcap ●x275
Headlamp lens ●x100 (independent)
Tail light assembly ●x540 (independent)

Ribbed tail lights expensive to replace if cracked. (Courtesy Artcurial Motorcars/ Christophe Gasco)

3 Living with a W116
– will you get along together?

Good points

One of the dealers specialising in the model described the W116 to the author as marking a "quantum leap" forward when compared to the W108/W109 models it replaced. In every respect, it was a far more sophisticated design, making it feel much more modern to drive. Its mechanical refinement and smoothness bring it closer to the W126 of the 1980s. It was planned from the outset to be fitted with V8 engines and these now had a 'proper' automatic gearbox using a torque converter rather than the fluid coupling of its predecessors. The suspension design was also highly advanced, ensuring much improved handling and an excellent ride. More sophisticated still, the 450 SEL 6.9 was in a class of its own when launched, and was, arguably, the best car in the world.

Although they may seem unyielding at first, the characteristically firm German seats provide great support on a long journey. Levels of equipment vary widely from car to car, but a well-optioned 450 SEL, for example, will have many of the features we now take for granted, such as air-conditioning, power-operated windows and a sunroof. All cars were extremely well finished, and the wool-rich velour or leather upholstery optioned on many cars give a genuine feeling of luxury.

Occupant safety was a major concern at the time the W116 was in development, and the model served as the basis for a series of experimental safety vehicles. It was one of the first production cars to offer ABS anti-lock braking as an

Space and luxury in this 450 SEL. (Courtesy Robin Adams ©2015 RM Sotheby's)

US-spec W116 with one of the experimental safety cars in the Mercedes museum.

Period press shot showing rare manual transmission. (Courtesy Mercedes-Benz Classic)

option (from 1978), developed jointly with Bosch. Its body was built around a safety cage structure with front and rear crumple zones, while the doors were designed to protect against side impacts. The fuel tank was positioned over the rear axle to shield it from damage in rear-end accidents.

Today, the car's advanced design and safety features make it a reassuring choice for would-be owners and their families, perhaps buying a classic car for the first time. And there are far fewer electronic components to go wrong than with the W126 or W140 series that followed.

Bad points
The sheer size of the W116 – especially in long-wheelbase guise – makes it better suited to motorways (freeways) and fast main roads than narrow country lanes or tight city streets. In standard-wheelbase form, however, the model is no more spacious inside than the earlier and more compact W108, as all the safety engineering features eat into the room available.

Living the good life: launch marketing for the 450 SEL 6.9.
(Courtesy Mercedes-Benz Classic)

In city use, the manual gearchange can seem cumbersome, especially in combination with Mercedes' traditional foot-operated parking brake.

Summary
With the exception of the mighty 6.9-litre flagship, the W116 is not a sporty car to drive; rather, it should be enjoyed for its comfort on the open road and the sense of occasion which any S-Class Mercedes confers on its passengers. Would-be buyers who put a premium on style may want to look instead at the SLC coupés from the same period, based on a lengthened version of the R107 SL platform.

Period press photo of all Mercedes' 450 models, including the SL and SLC.
(Courtesy Mercedes-Benz Classic)

Body styles

Mercedes-Benz only ever offered the W116 in saloon (sedan) guise, in either standard or long-wheelbase versions. The 280 S and US-market 300 SD came only in standard-wheelbase form, the 450 SEL 6.9 solely with the longer wheelbase. 292 armoured cars were built, but hopefully readers of this guide will not need that protection!

Other than its badge, the 6.9 had only marginally wider tyres and a speedo calibrated to 260km/h/170mph to distinguish it from the lesser models in the range, making it a real 'Q-car'!

Long-wheelbase versions offer extra rear seat legroom. (Courtesy Mercedes-Benz Classic)

Armoured versions had no rear quarter windows. (Courtesy Mercedes-Benz Classic)

The factory never offered an estate model (wagon), but several conversions were produced, notably by Crayford in the UK, using a tailgate from the Ford Granada. A handful of cars were also converted by German coachbuilders, while various companies in the US and Europe produced small numbers of stretch limos and hearses.

Which engine?

If you are already set on buying a 450 SEL 6.9, you can probably skip this section! The 6.9 used a development of the M100 engine originally fitted to the 600 'Grosser' Mercedes. It came with far more equipment as standard, especially in export markets, as well as unique features such as its self-levelling hydropneumatic suspension. A good 6.9, however, will cost at least twice as much as any other version, so if your budget won't stretch that far, keep reading …

Unless you really want a manual gearchange, it is tempting simply to recommend a 450 for the ultimate refinement they offer. They are powerful but still reasonably straightforward to maintain. There is much to be said, however, for buying on condition and history first, rather than on mechanical specification. Even the 280 SE can reach a top speed of 120mph (193km/h).

All the petrol engines were launched a year or so before the W116 was introduced, so any teething problems had been ironed out. With dual overhead camshafts, the 2.8-litre 'six' is a sporty unit that likes to rev. The carburettor-fed S model was not sold in the UK, but in any event, the fuel-injected SE is the better choice, for its smoother running and extra power. Its performance is close to that of the 350 SE, and in automatic form it had four speeds rather than three.

With little difference in prices between the two 'regular' V8s, there is a good case for choosing a 450 SE or 450 SEL over the smaller-engined 350 SE or SEL. Initially reserved for the US, this engine produced significantly more torque and is a long-lived, unstressed unit. Note that cars sold in North America generally produced less power and torque than those destined for Europe, due to the mandatory emissions equipment there.

The diesel-engined 300 SD was originally sold only in North America, in response to the CAFE legislation introduced in 1975 to fine car makers if the average fuel consumption of all their cars exceeded a set figure. A five-cylinder turbocharged three-litre engine developing 168lb/ft of torque ensured that performance remained acceptable. Well-equipped as standard, it proved quite successful, with 29,000 cars sold. Today, however, it is strictly a niche choice. A few cars have made their way to Europe, but with increasing restrictions on the use of older diesels in cities, it is hard to recommend them. Most potential buyers of the W116 will in any case prefer the refinement of the petrol-engined variants.

Which transmission?
The vast majority of W116s came with automatic transmission, with three or four speeds depending on the model. For most drivers, this is probably best suited to the cars' refined character. The selector for nearly all cars was in the centre console, but a few early cars may be found with a column-mounted shift lever.

The 280 S and SE came as standard, however, with a four-speed manual transmission (a five-speed was optional), and a four-speed manual was also offered on the 350 SE and SEL.

Early 280 SE automatic with column-mounted gear selector and single Zebrano wood trim strip on dashboard. (Courtesy Mercedes-Benz Classic)

Which year?
Unlike Mercedes' later models, which saw one or more major face-lifts, the W116 went through a process of continuous improvement. Over time, the list of standard or optional equipment was extended, with the addition of front and rear headrests, heated seats and more elaborate radios, while extra wood trim was added to the centre console.

In general, this approach makes choosing a particular year of production less

Later 450 SEL 6.9 has conventional transmission selector and extended burr walnut trim on centre console. (Courtesy Mercedes-Benz Classic)

important than the car's history and condition. One exception, however, concerns the fuel-injection system: by 1976, the mechanically-controlled Bosch K-Jetronic – which is cheaper to maintain – had replaced the earlier D-Jetronic system across the board.

The power output of cars sold in North America varied more year-to-year than in Europe, as a result of the emissions legislation there. From 1974 onwards, US models also had reinforced bumpers which added nearly 10in (25cm) to the cars' length and look very ungainly.

300 SD with US Federal-spec bumpers and round headlamps.
(Courtesy Mercedes-Benz Classic)

5 Before you view
– be well informed

To avoid a wasted journey, and the disappointment of finding that the car does not match your expectations, it will help if you're very clear about what questions you want to ask before you pick up the telephone. Some of these points might appear basic, but when you're excited about the prospect of buying your dream classic, it's amazing how some of the most obvious things slip the mind ... You can also check the current values of the model that attracts you in classic car magazines, which give both a price guide and auction results.

Where is the car?
Is it going to be worth travelling to the next county/state, or even across a border? A locally advertised car, although it may not sound very interesting, can add to your knowledge for very little effort, so make a visit – it might even be in better condition than expected.

Dealer or private sale
Establish early on if the car is being sold by its owner or by a trader. A private owner should have all the history, so don't be afraid to ask detailed questions. A dealer may have more limited knowledge of a car's history but should have some documentation. A dealer may offer a warranty/guarantee (ask for a printed copy) and finance.

Cost of collection and delivery
A dealer may well be used to quoting for delivery by car transporter. A private owner may agree to meet you halfway, but only agree to this after you have seen the car at the vendor's address to validate the documents. Alternatively, you could meet halfway and agree the sale but insist on meeting at the vendor's address for the handover.

View – when and where
It is always preferable to view at the vendor's home or business premises. In the case of a private sale, the car's documentation should tally with the vendor's name and address. Arrange to view only in daylight and avoid a wet day: most cars look better in poor light or when wet.

Reason for sale
Make it one of the first questions. Why is the car being sold and how long has it been with the current owner? How many previous owners?

Imports
As with nearly all German makes, you will find many more cars on sale in their home country than elsewhere. When you buy a car from another country, you may need to make changes to the number (license) plates, lighting (headlamps and indicators) and radio equipment. If you re-register a car from Germany or elsewhere in the EU in another country, you may need to obtain an attestation from Mercedes-Benz that it conforms to the original specification.

If the car is modified, do you even want to bother viewing it?
(Courtesy Tom Wood ©2018 RM Sotheby's)

Condition (body/chassis/interior/mechanicals)
Query the car's condition in as specific terms as possible – preferably citing the checklist items described in Chapter 9 – Serious evaluation.

All original specification
An original equipment car is invariably of higher value than a customised version.

Matching data/legal ownership
Do Vehicle Identification Number (VIN)/chassis, engine numbers and licence plate match the official registration document? Is the owner's name and address recorded in the official registration documents? For those countries that require an annual test of roadworthiness, does the car have a document showing it complies (an MOT certificate in the UK, which can be verified on www.gov.uk/check-mot-status)? If a smog/emissions certificate is mandatory, does the car have one? If required, does the car carry a current road fund licence/licence plate tag? Does the vendor own the

Compare the VIN on the paperwork with the plate on the car. (Courtesy Artcurial Motorcars/ Christophe Gasco)

car outright? Money might be owed to a finance company or bank: the car could even be stolen. Several organisations will supply the data on ownership, based on the car's licence plate number, for a fee. Such companies can often also tell you whether the car has been 'written-off' by an insurance company. In the UK, these organisations can supply vehicle data:
HPI – 0845 300 8905; www.hpi.co.uk/
AA – 0800 316 3564; www.theaa.com/
DVLA – 0300 790 6802; www.gov.uk/get-vehicle-information-from-dvla/
RAC – 0330 058 9349; www.rac.co.uk/
Other countries will have similar organisations.

Insurance
Check with your existing insurer before setting out, as your current policy might not cover you to drive the car if you do purchase it.

How you can pay
A cheque (check) will take several days to clear and the seller may prefer to sell to a cash buyer. However, a banker's draft (a cheque issued by a bank) is as good as cash, but safer, so contact your own bank and become familiar with the formalities that are necessary to obtain one.

Buying at auction?
If the intention is to buy at auction, see Chapter 10 – Auctions for further advice.

Professional vehicle check (mechanical examination)
There are often marque/model specialists who will undertake professional examination of a vehicle on your behalf. Owners clubs will be able to put you in touch with such specialists. Other motoring organisations with vehicle inspectors that will carry out a general professional check in the UK are:
AA – 0800 056 8040; www.theaa.com/
RAC – 0330 159 1111; www.rac.co.uk/
Other countries will have similar organisations.

6 Inspection equipment
– these items will really help

This book
Reading glasses (if you need them for close work)
Torch
Magnet (not powerful, a fridge magnet is ideal)
Probe (a small screwdriver works very well)
Overalls
Mirror on a stick
Digital camera (or smartphone)
A friend, preferably a knowledgeable enthusiast

This book is designed to be your guide at every step, so take it along and use the check boxes to help you assess each area of the car you're interested in. Don't be afraid to let the seller see you using it.

Take your reading glasses if you need them to read documents and make close-up inspections.

A torch with fresh batteries will be useful for peering into the wheelarches and under the car.

A magnet will help you check if the car is full of filler. Use the magnet to sample bodywork areas all around the car but be careful not to damage the paintwork. Expect to find a little filler here and there, but not whole panels.

A small screwdriver can be used – with care – as a probe, particularly in the wheelarches and on the underside. With this you should be able to check an area of

The engine bay on a well-travelled car like this will need a close inspection.

severe corrosion, but be careful – if it's really bad, the screwdriver might go right through the metal!

Be prepared to get dirty. Take along a pair of overalls, if you have them.

Fixing a mirror at an angle on the end of a stick may seem odd, but you'll probably need it to check the condition of the underside of the car. It will also help

A screwdriver will help you check the extent of rust in places, such as under this fuel filler.

you to peer into some of the important crevices. You can also use it, together with the torch, along the underside of the sills and on the floor.

If you have a digital camera or smartphone, take it along so that later you can study some areas of the car more closely. Take a picture of any part of the car that causes you concern and seek a friend's opinion. Like the mirror on a stick, a 'selfie stick' may help you get your smartphone under the car.

Ideally, have a friend or knowledgeable enthusiast accompany you: a second opinion is always valuable.

7 Fifteen minute evaluation
– walk away or stay?

The W116 was a sophisticated car when new, but with relatively few good cars left, it is more important than ever to assess each example with care. There were no major face-lifts during the series' life cycle, so the points below apply equally to all years of production and to each model in the range.

Exterior

As you approach the car for the first time, check that it sits level and square on the road. On 6.9 models with self-levelling suspension, make sure that the car settles at the correct height with the engine running.

Only the badge at the rear differentiates the various models. (Courtesy Bonhams)

Unless it has been recently restored, some minor scrapes are almost inevitable on a car of this age, but dented panels, scuffed alloy wheels and ancient or badly worn tyres all point to a lack of care. The W116 has plenty of attractive chrome trim: if any of these parts, such as the bumpers or radiator cowling,

The rear bumper, sill and wheel can all tell you a lot about the car's overall condition.

are in poor condition, refurbishing them will be costly.

Rust is the biggest bugbear afflicting the W116. If you are looking at a car in a wet or snowy area – especially if salt is used on the roads in winter – it is all the more likely to be affected. While rust also occurs around the windows or sunroof aperture, the worst corrosion is usually found lower down, at the base of the sills and along the bottom of the doors. Get down on the ground to check these areas of the body and, if possible, take a look underneath: rust to the rear suspension trailing arms, for instance, is potentially lethal. Are there any indications that a tow bar has been fitted? The extra load of towing a caravan or boat may have put additional strain on the transmission and brakes.

Assuming that the body is not badly corroded (in which case a respray may be needed anyway after it has been repaired), step back to look at the paintwork. Does it appear uniform across the different panels? Are there signs of fading, particularly if you are viewing a car from a hot, sunny area?

Is all the chrome trim present and correct? (Courtesy GGE Classic)

This sunroof has rusted badly; check for stains and leaks inside, too.

Interior and boot (trunk)
All S-Class cars were built to rack up the miles, often at high speed. Look for signs of hard use such as smooth patches on the steering wheel rim or gear knob, or

excessive wear on the pedal rubbers, and check the mileage recorded on service documents or inspection certificates for any discrepancies.

The interior of the W116 is essentially very durable, especially when trimmed with the basic MB-Tex (vinyl). The luxurious velour upholstery, however, is more liable to wear and fading. Lighter colours show the dirt more easily. Look for cracks to the plastic on the top of the dashboard and any missing items of trim, which may be hard to replace. Are there any cracks in the wood veneer along the dashboard and on the centre console? Mercedes' seats were traditionally very firm and should remain supportive; if not, the springs may have collapsed, particularly on the driver's side, and the seats will need to be rebuilt.

Lift the carpets and check for signs of dampness due to water leaks. On cars with sunroofs, inspect the headlining for water stains. If left untreated, these leaks will quickly allow rust to set in. Rust can also take hold in the boot, so be sure to lift up the floor covering and remove the spare wheel to look carefully inside.

With the ignition key turned to the accessory position, turn on the lights and see whether the dashboard lighting works as it should. When

Does the engine appear to have been regularly maintained? (Courtesy Bonhams)

you start the engine – after waiting for the glow plugs on the 300 SD – check that all the warning lights go out. Do all the lights, including those for the rear number plate, work correctly? There are relatively few electrical items to check on a W116, but make sure that any optional equipment functions normally. This applies especially to cars fitted with air-conditioning: the push button controls on the climate control system fitted from 1976 are notoriously troublesome.

The engine compartment and underbody
The engine compartment need not be immaculately clean (in fact, that might even look suspicious!) and evidence of minor oil leaks is not necessarily alarming. Larger spills or a tell-tale patch beneath the car are more worrisome, as are light-coloured stains suggesting a coolant leak. Are the different hoses and the sound insulation pad in good condition, or have they dried out and cracked? If you can get underneath the car, have a look at the various rubber suspension bushings.

Modifications
Aftermarket parts, such as body dress-up kits, are largely a matter of personal taste. Most enthusiasts, however, will prefer original, unmodified cars and these will normally be easier to sell on. If you do go for a car with modified bodywork or interior trim, there are two important things to consider. First, can the parts fitted be easily changed back to standard (assuming those parts are still available)? And secondly, are they professionally fitted and still in good condition? Some add-on

parts – such as chrome wheelarch extensions – can create problems of their own as they harbour rust. Mechanical upgrades to the W116 are rare, but if the performance has been increased, you should check whether the brakes and suspension have been uprated to match.

An Italian-style wheel may jar but can easily be replaced.
(Courtesy Robin Adams ©2015 RM Sotheby's)

Is it genuine and legal?

However attractive the car may look at first, it's essential that the paperwork is in order. First of all, does the VIN (the 17-digit Vehicle Identification Number) on the car tally with that on the registration/title document? On the W116, you will find the VIN on a plate riveted on the bonnet slam panel and stamped on the bulkhead

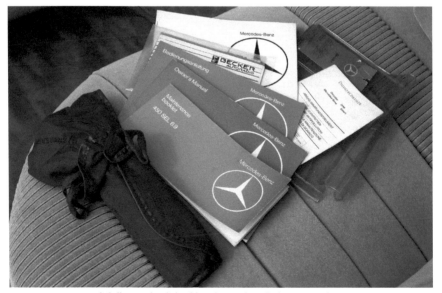

A full set of original books and tools is reassuring.
(Courtesy Artcurial Motorcars/Christophe Gasco)

at the back of the engine bay. Make sure that the VIN hasn't been tampered with and take a note or photograph of it for reference. You can look up the VIN online to confirm the year of manufacture and specification of the car you are considering.

Independent organisations (see Chapter 5 – Before you view) will let you check that there is no finance outstanding on the car and no record of serious accident damage. Does the seller's name and address appear on the registration or title document? If you are buying privately, be sure to view the car at the owner's home address, so that you can check this tallies with the paperwork for the car. If something doesn't seem right here, walk away now. At best, you may have problems registering the car; at worst, it may be stolen or unroadworthy.

Only buy a car from an individual who can prove that they are the person named in the car's registration document and, preferably, at the address shown in the document.

If all these details are correct, ask to see details of the car's service history including, if possible, invoices for work done, showing the parts which have been replaced. Don't be put off by stamps in the service book or invoices from independent specialists: they often have more expertise in working on cars from this era than official Mercedes-Benz dealerships. Sometimes, however, the reason for sale will be less encouraging. There may be a big repair job looming, or the seller may have run out of time or money to complete a restoration.

If the car requires an annual roadworthiness certificate in your country (such as the MOT test in the UK), make sure that this is current, and note any advisories, indicating work that should be done. These may not be reason enough to reject the car, you may be able to negotiate a reduction in the price or ask the seller to include some spare parts in the deal. Finally, make sure that the mileage on the car's odometer matches that on the service documentation or test certificates.

Road test

This preliminary inspection will probably have given you a good idea of whether the car is worth further consideration. Before you embark on a longer examination, now is a good time to see how the car drives. Even if you feel that a car is outside your budget, it is worth driving at least one really decent W116, to give you a bench mark of just how good a W116 can be. Even poor cars will drive quite well, which can trick you into overlooking their faults.

If the seller refuses to take the car out or let you drive, be ready to turn away. A road test taking in a variety of city traffic, open roads and motorways (freeways) is essential to assessing any car. Before starting off, check that the insurance covers you to drive, and that the indicators, lights and wipers all work. Try and start the engine from cold if possible: it should start readily and idle smoothly. As soon as you open the throttle, the oil pressure gauge should move to its maximum reading (3bar). On cars with fuel-injection, try starting the engine when it is warm as well, for example at the end of your test drive.

Keep the radio off and listen out for any untoward noises. The overall impression should be one of comfort and mechanical quietness. If the car runs unevenly, it may just be a worn distributor cap or rotor arm (which are cheap and easy to replace), or there may be a more serious fault with the fuel system. A loud knocking noise when accelerating may signal a damaged conrod or worn main bearings. Look out too for blue smoke from the exhaust, which may be the result of worn piston rings or valve guides. Excessive wind noise often occurs when the window seals have perished.

Keep an eye on the temperature gauge (around 80°C is normal on the open road); if the car begins to overheat in traffic, it may have too little coolant or a blocked radiator. If the speedometer needle flickers, the cable may just need regreasing. A flickering fuel gauge needle, on the other hand, may be the result of a faulty sender. Incidentally, some basic-spec cars came with a large clock on the right of the instrument panel and no rev counter.

On a clear stretch of open road, take your hands off the steering wheel: the car should continue to run straight. If it doesn't, an alignment check may be required. Some free play in the steering (a maximum of two fingers) is considered normal, but more than this will mean that adjustment or an overhaul of the steering will be needed. If you feel any knocking or vibration with the steering at full lock, the engine mounts may be worn.

All versions of the W116 should offer a comfortable ride, but none more so than the 450 SEL 6.9 with its hydropneumatic self-levelling suspension. A choppy ride on a 6.9 most likely means that the suspension spheres need to be refilled or even replaced. You should also check that the ride height can be adjusted (using the knob under the instrument cluster).

If the car you are testing is fitted with automatic transmission, forward and reverse drive should both engage cleanly, although a pause of a couple of seconds is normal when shifting from reverse into drive. All changes should be reasonably smooth, whether made automatically, using kickdown or the manual override; the older four-speed automatic fitted to the 280 S/SE was never as smooth, however, as the later torque converter type.

On cars fitted with manual transmission, make sure that the clutch engages and disengages smoothly with no judder. The gearchange is naturally notchy, but you should be able to select all gears without any untoward noises or obstruction. Check for

Check that the automatic transmission shifts cleanly. (Courtesy Bonhams)

A 350 SE at speed on the open road. (Courtesy Mercedes-Benz Classic)

any signs of clutch slip and weak synchromesh, particularly when engaging second gear.

When traffic conditions allow, apply the brakes hard: the car should pull up straight. Any judder means that the discs (rotors) are warped or corroded and should be replaced. On late-model cars fitted with the optional anti-lock brakes (ABS), you should feel the pedal pulsing as the system operates. Try to test the parking brake on an incline, to ensure that it will hold the car securely.

Exterior
- Are all the panels straight, with even gaps?
- Are there signs of corrosion, particularly on the wings, doors and sills and around the sunroof (if fitted)?
- Is the chrome trim complete and in good condition?
- Are the seals for the doors and windows in good order?

The rear wing, wheelarch and sill are all potential rust spots.

Are the big chrome bumpers and radiator cowling still in good condition? (Courtesy GGE Classic)

Interior
• Does the overall condition of the interior appear consistent with the mileage shown?
• Can you see or smell any signs of damp under the carpets or stains on the headlining (especially if a sunroof is fitted)?
• Is the upholstery (particularly velour) in good condition, or is it faded and worn?
• Is any of the plastic or wood trim cracked or missing?
• If air-conditioning is fitted, does this still work properly?

Engine and mechanicals
• Does the engine compartment appear clean, without any major oil or coolant leaks?
• Are the different hoses and wires secure and in good condition?
• Does the engine run smoothly, without blue or black smoke from the exhaust?
• On the 450 SEL 6.9, does the suspension rise up correctly when the car is started? Does the car sit level?
• If you can look underneath, are the chassis and suspension free from rust?
• Is there a service history with the car?

The engine of this 450 SEL 6.9 has been thoroughly overhauled prior to sale. (Courtesy GGE Classic)

9 Serious evaluation
– 60 minutes for years of enjoyment

If you've come this far, well done! The paperwork is in order and the car looks promising. Now is the time to take a really thorough look over it, bearing in mind the points already mentioned in the last two chapters. Try and work your way systematically around the car, so that you don't miss any details. Start outside with a close look at the bodywork, before turning your attention to the interior and finally the engine and underbody.

Score each section using the boxes as follows:
4 = excellent; 3 = good; 2 = average; 1 = poor. The totting-up procedure is detailed at the end of the chapter. Be realistic in your marking!

Exterior
First impressions

Make sure that you can view the car outdoors and in daylight, preferably in good weather. The car should be clean; it's hard to judge the condition of paint under a layer of dirt or dust.

Rust bubbles and uneven bumpers don't make for a good start.

Begin by stepping back from the car: does it appear to sag on either side or at one end?

Has the car been modified in any way? If larger wheels have been fitted, do they still clear the wheelarches, especially on full lock? Are any accessory body parts fitted? If so, make a note to check carefully that they are securely attached and not concealing any rust.

Bodywork

Look at the overall condition of the body: are the panels straight and free from dents? When you look along the side of the car, does anything seem out of line? The panel gaps should be consistent right around the car. The complex crumple zones in the structure of the W116 make it harder to repair the car well after a major accident, so it is especially important to check for misaligned panels and mismatched paint.

Poor repairs may be disguised with filler or hidden beneath layers of

Check along the car for straight panels with even gaps.

underseal: don't be afraid to probe any suspect areas with a small magnet. Model badges attached in the wrong position on the boot (trunk) lid often give away a previous accident repair. Check the roof too, for signs of hailstone damage.

Make a point of opening the boot and each of the doors in turn: even on well-maintained cars, the seals may have hardened with age and will eventually let in moisture, allowing corrosion to take hold.

Body corrosion 4 3 2 1

The W116 is such a strong car mechanically that body corrosion stands out even more as the key issue to look out for. Unlike the later W126, the bodyshells of the W116 were not galvanised. All cars – and especially those built prior to 1976 – are highly vulnerable to rust. Although it is hard to find a W116 which has not had some welding work done on it, look for a car which is as original and rust-free as possible.

These door rubbers are in a sorry state, with the first signs of rust apparent.

Corrosion evident along the base of this door and wing.

Perished rubber and rust forming above this rear light unit.

The W116 rusts pretty much everywhere, so take your time and work your way around the car. The doors, bonnet (hood) and boot (trunk) lid all corrode. The doors should be examined at the bottom and around the window frames; on the bonnet, pay particular attention to the leading edge, where damage from stone chips may have been left unchecked. The bonnet and boot lid on the 300 SD were made from aluminium, so there is an additional risk of contact corrosion.

The wings and wheelarches (especially at the rear, where rust typically starts at the bottom) should be checked thoroughly. Run your hand around the inside of each wheelarch to check for patches of rust. Be wary of chrome wheelarch trims – more often found on cars for sale in North America – as these can trap moisture and hide signs of corrosion.

The lower, more modern styling of the W116 meant that it had a smaller radiator grille than the W108/W109 and required a large air inlet below the front bumper. The front apron and the crossmember behind it both rust, but sometimes this is limited to surface corrosion, which can be treated quite easily.

Other areas to check include the rear apron and the edges of the front and rear screens and sunroof (if fitted). Finally, don't forget to open the fuel filler cap (which should have a tyre pressure sticker inside it).

If you are particularly concerned about the condition of certain parts of the body, it's worth investigating whether replacements are still available. Major panels such as the bonnet, boot lid, front door or rear wing, for example, are no longer available from Mercedes, so you will need to turn to independent specialists to locate NOS (new old stock) or secondhand parts.

Chassis and sills

Mercedes only began to use cavity wax treatments after 1980, so the rocker panels and jacking points on the W116 are more vulnerable to corrosion. If the outer sills show signs of rust, it is likely that the inner sections will also be affected and will require a potentially expensive repair.

Inside the car, lift up the carpet in each footwell to check for signs of dampness, which will then cause the floor to rust. Cars fitted with sunroofs are particularly prone to this, as blocked drainage channels can cause water to leak into the car. If you can look at the car on a lift, that will give you a further opportunity

It is rare to see a rear wheelarch in such superb condition as this.

This sill is already rusting right through.

Well-filled 6.9 engine bay needs to be examined carefully.

to assess the condition of the floor.

Under the bonnet (hood)

With the bonnet open, inspect the inner wings and the spot where these meet the bulkhead. Blocked drains and condensation can frequently result in corrosion at the front and back of the bulkhead. Look carefully for any corrosion behind the heater blower cover

Look under the battery for signs of acid leakage and corrosion.

(ask the seller if you may remove this to check). Major rust damage to the bulkhead is a serious issue and you should be ready to walk away.

Looking right down inside the engine compartment, check the lower front crossmember, the front chassis rails and the front suspension mounts (including the top of the suspension towers) for evidence of corrosion. Acid leaks can also cause the battery tray to rust.

Chrome and other trim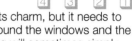

The W116's abundant chrome trim is an essential part of its charm, but it needs to have been well looked after. The door handles, the trim around the windows and the side rubbing strips should all be checked. Superficial pitting will sometimes simply polish out, but that will not always be enough.

The two-tier front and rear bumpers are particularly distinctive, but over time the rubber inserts perish and come away, letting moisture get in and rust to start. (The same can also happen with the side rubbing strips.) If a replacement is needed, the main bumper sections are now hard to find. The big Federal-spec bumpers fitted

This door handle shows signs of pitting.

The rubber trim on this bumper is lifting, allowing in moisture.

to US-market cars, however, were made from stainless steel, so that is one less thing to worry about! The main cowling for the big chrome radiator grille is no longer stocked by Mercedes but can be obtained from independent specialists. At over ●x640, however, it is far from cheap.

Wheels

Many W116s came as standard with simple body-colour hubcaps and many enthusiasts love their classic look. If they need to be repainted, a special kit is available to make the job easier and the UK Mercedes-Benz Club has published a practical guide to the job. Using a sponge and warm water rather than a power washer will keep them looking good.

The same design of alloy wheel was offered across the range.

Standard-fit painted hubcap.

In the US and on the top-end models sold in Europe, it is more common to find the Fuchs alloy wheels (sometimes nicknamed 'Mexican hat' alloys). Neither type of wheel presents any major problems, but, like any alloy wheels, they can suffer from kerbing damage or go dull over time. Some US customers had the alloy wheels chrome-plated: this is a matter of individual taste, but you should check that the chrome plating is still intact.

Glass

④ ③ ② ①

Examine the windscreen, side windows and rear screen in turn. If any of the windows have been tinted, is the depth of tint within the legally allowable limits in your country? Is the film used still in good condition?

The condition of the windscreen is especially important, as it is most likely to be damaged by stone chips. A crack in the driver's line of sight may cause the car to fail a roadworthiness inspection such as the MOT test in the UK. Replacement screens are still available from Mercedes-Benz and could be used as a bargaining point if the car looks good otherwise.

Examine the seals carefully on all the windows: inevitably, these will perish over time. The seals will then let in water, causing corrosion around the front and rear screens or inside the door panels. Milky edges around the front and rear screens are a clear indication that water has leaked in at some point. If the rubber seals around the rear screen have dried out, they can let water leak into the boot.

Milky edge to the windscreen a clear sign that water has got in.

Sunroof

④ ③ ② ①

On cars without air-conditioning, a sunroof can be a real boon in hot weather. But it can also cause additional problems (so score four points if the car you are looking at is not fitted with one!). The felt around the outer edges of the sunroof panel can lift, letting in water and enabling corrosion to begin around the frame and the sliding

44

mechanism. Check the condition of the drainage channels too: if they are not kept clear, water can leak into the car, resulting in damp carpets and a rusty floor underneath. Replacing the complete sunroof assembly is an intricate and therefore costly job, and in extreme cases a rotten sunroof can be a deal breaker.

A nasty case of corrosion around the edge of this sunroof panel.

Interior
First impressions

For a luxury model like the S-Class, an interior in good condition can really add to your enjoyment of the car. Missing or damaged trim can be expensive to replace and sometimes hard to find, especially in less common colours.

If the car smells musty inside as you open the door, be particularly wary and lift up the carpets (and any overmats fitted) to look for further signs of dampness. It can

The blue velour interior on this 450 SEL 6.9 remains in superb condition. (Courtesy Artcurial Motorcars/ Dirk de Jager)

be hard to track down the cause of dampness: blocked sunroof drainage channels, perished door seals or a rusty heater plenum chamber can all end up letting in water.

Are the carpets still clean and in good condition? Good-quality replacement floor mats (using the original patterns) are available from independent specialists such as Classic Mercedes Mats (www.classicmercedesmats.co.uk/).

As you get behind the wheel, look carefully at the steering wheel, gear knob and pedal rubbers: if these seem shiny and heavily worn, the car has probably covered a high mileage. Does that match the distance showing on the odometer?

If the door seals have dried out, replacements are no longer available from Mercedes, but independent specialists such as Niemöller can supply them (with a set costing ●x300).

Seats and upholstery

Mercedes offered a variety of different materials for the seats in the W116. The standard upholstery – most commonly found on 280 S/SE models and earlier 350 SE cars, especially in Germany – was the textured vinyl known as MB-Tex or a simple cloth trim to the centre panels with MB-Tex side sections. Lighter colours show the dirt more, but the MB-Tex trim is legendary for its durability and will usually respond well to a thorough clean. On cars with part vinyl/part cloth upholstery, the seams between the different sections can come undone.

Leather and velour upholstery add a feeling of luxury and 'lift' the interior. The

Don't hesitate to lift any overmats fitted to check the carpet and floorpan underneath.
(Courtesy Erik Fuller ©2017 RM Sotheby's)

Light-coloured upholstery and headlining is particularly vulnerable to staining. (Courtesy Edward Hall)

'Pullman'-style velour trim, with ribbed outer sections to the seats, was considered the height of luxury in Germany when the cars were new, and it is particularly comfortable in cold weather. The US and other export markets often preferred leather, however, and this is easier to recondition. On velour-trimmed cars, look for signs of wear, especially on the driver's seat side bolster, and for fading, in particular on the top of the rear bench. Cars from hot and sunny countries or states are especially prone to fading, but the velour can also rot if the car has become damp.

Replacement seat covers are of variable quality, but the seats can be re-trimmed in the different materials which were offered from new. Be sure, however, to use a good-quality specialist who is familiar with Mercedes' classics, such as d:class automotive in the UK (www.dclass.co.uk/). Experts like these will also be able to help if the seat bases have collapsed.

Finally, take a look up at the headlining: is it clean and free from stains? A sagging headlining is a problem which besets many older cars and not just the W116, but replacing it is a fiddly, time-consuming job that many mechanics would prefer to avoid.

Trim   4   3   2   1

The W116's excellent build quality helps the cars to age well inside. Inevitably though, the hard plastics used can become brittle over time and the trim can crack, especially on the top of the dashboard when the cars are exposed to the sun in hotter climates. Blue trim is particularly vulnerable to UV rays.

Check for damage caused by poorly installed audio equipment (including holes left by speakers in the door cards and rear parcel shelf) or mobile phone and satnav holders attached to the centre console.

Originally, the cars had a single strip of Zebrano wood trim on the dashboard, which was later extended down the centre console. The 450 SEL 6.9, however, had

Check the door cards are intact and the covering still taut.

This 1980 450 SEL has Zebrano wood trim right down the centre console. (Courtesy Bonhams)

much more lavish burr walnut trim. Whichever is fitted to the car you are viewing, check that it is complete and free from cracks; existing trim can be refurbished, but replacement parts can be hard to source, and it can be difficult to match the grain and colour of the wood.

In the rear compartment, look to see if the first-aid kit is still present in the compartment under the parcel shelf. Are the luggage nets on the back of the front seats still in place and taut? These often sag if overfilled.

Luggage compartment

As with the interior, it is crucial to check for signs of damp in the luggage area. The rubber seals around the rear screen can perish and let in water. Check the floor covering for signs of damp; a

The hazard warning triangle should be clipped to the inside of the boot lid. (Courtesy Mercedes-Benz Classic)

missing or brand-new carpet may also be suspicious. Lift it up and examine the floor for evidence of corrosion, especially inside the spare wheel well. The seller should not object to your lifting out the spare wheel and having a close look into the recesses. The cars were delivered with a hazard warning triangle clipped to the inside of the boot lid: is this still present?

Spotless spare wheel bay and original Michelin-shod alloy.
(©2018 Courtesy RM Auctions)

Electrics
Instruments and controls ☐4 ☐3 ☐2 ☐1

In general, the W116 had far fewer electrical fittings to give trouble than later S-Class models. Many cars, especially the 280 S and SE models, had manual window winders, and even on the 450 SEL 6.9 the seat adjustment was manual. Each item of equipment should nonetheless be tested in turn. Make sure that the

Classic three-dial Mercedes instrument cluster, with 260km/h speedometer in 6.9.
(Courtesy Tom Wood ©2018 RM Sotheby's)

rotary knob for the lights and the combination switch on the steering column (for main beam, wipers and indicators) work correctly.

Cars sold new in the US had more standard equipment than in Europe, with cruise control (known as 'Tempomat') introduced there in 1974, two years before it became available in Europe. The 300 SD was sold 'fully loaded' and came with power windows, a radio and air-conditioning as standard, while the 450 SEL 6.9 often had more extras specified when new.

Audio systems

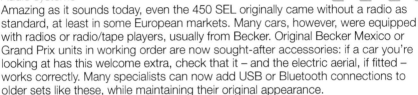

Amazing as it sounds today, even the 450 SEL originally came without a radio as standard, at least in some European markets. Many cars, however, were equipped with radios or radio/tape players, usually from Becker. Original Becker Mexico or Grand Prix units in working order are now sought-after accessories: if a car you're looking at has this welcome extra, check that it – and the electric aerial, if fitted – works correctly. Many specialists can now add USB or Bluetooth connections to older sets like these, while maintaining their original appearance.

Highly prized Becker Mexico AM/FM radio and cassette deck. (Courtesy Erik Fuller ©2017 RM Sotheby's)

Lights

Cars originally sold in Europe had horizontal front lamp units, incorporating halogen headlamps and front foglights, while US cars were fitted with dual round sealed-beam headlights and separate foglights under the bumper. There are few problems here specific to the W116 with either set-up, but the lenses should be checked for cracks and stone chips.

The rear lights – which at ●x540 are expensive to replace – should also be examined: as with all Mercedes models from this period, they were ribbed to

Top: European-style headlamps, with yellow lenses on this French-market car. (Courtesy Artcurial Motorcars/Dirk de Jager) Below: Dual round headlamps on the US models. (Courtesy Bonhams)

prevent dirt building up in bad weather. If the seals perish, the metal around them can corrode and water may leak into the boot.

Air-conditioning

Score four points if not fitted, for reasons which will become clear …

As is often the case with Mercedes, the standard heating and ventilation system (using an air-blending heater with separate controls for driver and front-seat passenger) is excellent. The cars even featured special ducts to channel hot air to the inner skin of the doors.

The fitment of air-conditioning is a mixed blessing. Pre-76 cars had a manual Behr air-conditioning system, after which a more complex climate control system became available. This had more than its share of problems, even when the cars were new, with the servo seals splitting open and leaking coolant. As the cars have aged, the push-button controls may stop working, while the blower motor can fail after the contact brushes wear out.

Whichever system is fitted, check which refrigerant is used (there should be a sticker on the slam panel under the bonnet); R12 was originally used but this has now been banned. Substitutes such as Duracool exist, so you may still be able to use the original system if it is continuing to operate correctly. If the air-conditioning is not blowing properly cold air, however, and a simple recharge is not enough, you will need to overhaul the system so that it can use the now current R134a refrigerant.

This is an expensive job which must be performed by an A/C specialist. The seals and pipes will need to be replaced; after 40 years or more, it is very likely that components such as the condenser and compressor will need to be overhauled as well.

AUTOMOTIVE AIR CONDITIONER	R 12 max.
CONFORMS TO SAE J 639	107/201
KLIMAANLAGE FÜR AUTOMOBILE	1.0 kg 2.2 lbs
AUSFÜHRUNG NACH SAE J 639	
DAIMLER-Benz AG	123/126
STUTTGART · UNTERTÜRKHEIM	1.3 kg 2.9 lbs
	124
124 835 01 88	1.1 kg 2.4 lbs

Under bonnet sticker specifies type and quantity of refrigerant.

Later push-button type climate control can be problematic. (Courtesy Erik Fuller ©2017 RM Sotheby's)

Battery

Use a multimeter to check the condition of the battery. Ask the seller when the battery was last changed and, if necessary, budget on getting a new one. Modern batteries are far more efficient than those fitted when the cars were new, and – unless you are aiming for concours-level originality – represent a wise investment, especially if you plan on only using the car occasionally. A trickle charger will also help keep the battery in good condition.

Engine and mechanicals
Under the bonnet (hood): first impressions

Start by lifting the bonnet right up to gain an overall impression of how the car has been looked after. Are there any traces of oil or other fluid leaks? As on many older Mercedes, there may be some minor oil seepage, but major leaks (around

A first look will often tell you how well a car has been maintained.
(Courtesy Bonhams)

the engine or underneath the car) should alert you to a more serious problem. Examine the condition of the fuel and brake lines and of the different hoses and accessory drivebelt: it is natural for rubber to dry out and perish over time, but these parts should have been replaced as part of an ongoing maintenance

Look for signs of wear on the accessory drivebelt.

programme. Beware of any smells of fuel, which may betray leaking fuel pipes.

Are there any signs of frayed or poorly insulated wires, which could represent a fire risk? Loose wires may be the result of accessories such as aftermarket alarms that have been fitted without proper care.

Radiators often rust over time, restricting the flow of coolant and so increasing the risk of overheating. Does the radiator core appear intact? If the radiator has been replaced, check to see whether the different hoses and fittings were changed at the same time.

The insulation pad disintegrates naturally over time and replacing it is a straightforward and inexpensive job. If it is already missing, you may see signs of rust on the underside of the bonnet, but this is usually only surface corrosion and not unduly worrisome. You may see surface corrosion on the exhaust manifolds as well, but again this is not normally a significant issue.

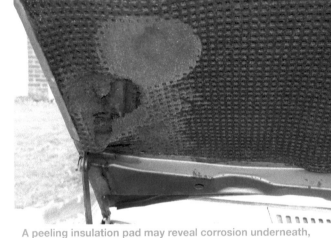

A peeling insulation pad may reveal corrosion underneath, but it is not always serious.

General mechanical issues

In general, all the engines and transmissions fitted to the W116 range are solidly engineered and very reliable, provided they have been regularly serviced. None of the petrol engines were originally designed to run on lead-free fuel. A lead replacement additive should therefore be used, unless hardened valve seats have been fitted as part of

M117 4.5-litre V8 in a US-spec 450 SEL from 1980.
(Courtesy Erik Fuller ©2017 RM Sotheby's)

an engine rebuild. Frequent oil changes will keep the engines well lubricated, while new air and fuel filters should be fitted regularly, and the coolant and sparkplugs changed. The failure to use the correct coolant, for example, can lead to corroded cylinder heads. Can the seller show you bills to confirm that these jobs have been done? Many of these are straightforward jobs for a home mechanic, and helpful guides are available online (see Chapter 16 – The Community). The timing chains rarely break but should be replaced every 100,000 miles as a precaution. Over time, the engine and transmission mounts can wear and should also be replaced.

Score only one of the three following sections (on the usual 4-3-2-1 scale) depending on which engine is fitted to the car you are assessing.

Six-cylinder petrol engines

The six-cylinder M110 engine is prone to oil leaks from the front and rear crankshaft seals and camshaft box, so take care to look for these. Remove the oil filler cap and check for signs of a mayonnaise-like deposit, which may indicate that the cylinder head gasket has failed, allowing oil and water to mix. There is a risk of both the fuel pump relay and oil pump failing: recent bills for replacement parts should reassure you that any problems have been addressed.

With the engine running, start by checking the oil pressure: the needle should show 2bar at idle and move right to the top of the scale (3bar) when you give the engine some revs. Look in the mirror for blue smoke from the exhaust, which may point to worn piston rings, and listen for the clatter of noisy valve gear higher up the rev range. Dealing with these issues will likely require an expensive mechanical overhaul.

On the 280 S, incorrect adjustment of the Solex 4A down-draft carburettor can often cause starting problems (hot and cold) and/or hesitation and flat spots. The

M110 unit from 280 on the left and M116 from 350 on the right.
(Courtesy Mercedes-Benz Classic)

engine is naturally quite thirsty and problems with the carburettor will also increase the fuel consumption still further; these may be evident from black smoke from the exhaust. As with the 250 and 280 models in the W123 range, adjusting this type of carburettor requires specialist knowledge and experience.

Most of the six-cylinder cars sold outside Germany, however, were equipped with fuel-injection: initially the electronic Bosch D-Jetronic system and then, from February 1976, the mechanical K-Jetronic set-up. If the car idles unevenly, this is often due to a problem with the fuel-injection.

The earlier D-Jetronic is prone to faults with the metering system and engine warm-up regulator. The laptop-sized ECU (Electric Control Unit) on this controls the injector opening time and supplies an earth feed for the fuel pump relay, which is liable to fail. It is, however, a complex system that requires specialist expertise to repair and maintain.

The later K-Jetronic type, which was integrated with the ignition system, has proven more reliable and replacement parts for it are cheaper. The type M110 engine used in the 280 SE and SEL continued to give faithful service in Mercedes' G-Wagen until 1990.

V8 petrol engines (including 6.9)

All the V8-engined cars (including the 6.9) came only with fuel-injection. The mechanical K-Jetronic system replaced the electronic D-Jetronic on the 450 SE/ SEL in November 1975 and on the 350 models in January 1976. All the 6.9 models were fitted with the later K-Jetronic set-up. The same caveats therefore apply to the fuel system on these models as on the six-cylinder petrol-engined cars.

The M116 unit on the 350 SE/SEL and the M117 on the 450 SE/SEL are generally smooth-running engines which should give excellent service if well looked after. Missed oil changes may result in wear to the camshaft and tappets (which will sound unduly noisy). The fuel pump has been known to leak on all models, and on pre-1976 cars, look too for leaks from the fuel hoses, especially at the rear of the engine.

Regular maintenance of the valve train is especially important with these engines: the valves should be adjusted every 15,000 miles and the timing chain checked for signs of excessive stretch or wear. Blue smoke from the exhaust when decelerating is a sign that the valve guides are worn. Although it may go on for longer, it is good preventive maintenance to change the timing chain every 100,000 miles, along with the tensioners, upper guides and cam gears. Replacing the valve guides is a complex and expensive job requiring the

The 4.5-litre V8 offered significantly more torque than the 3.5. (Courtesy Mercedes-Benz Classic)

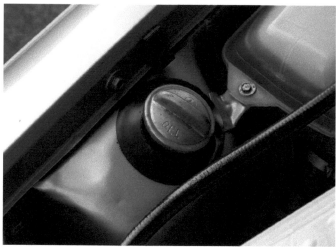

The oil filler for the 6.9 is located on the upper front wing.

removal of the cylinder heads; the complete operation can take 20-25 hours. If this work is needed on a car you are considering, remember to factor in the cost of the work when negotiating.

On early examples of the 350 SE and SEL, some cars suffered from a choke air speed problem, causing poor engine warm-up behaviour; the fuel-injection system was modified at the end of 1977 to overcome this.

On US-specification 450 SE and SEL models from 1975 and 1976, the catalytic converter was poorly positioned, causing vapour lock as the fuel started to boil, and made it hard to restart the engine. From 1977, the catalytic converter was relocated, and this change should have been made to all cars by now.

Finally, a word about the 450 SEL 6.9. This used a version of the M100 engine developed for the 600 'Grosser Mercedes' but enlarged to 6.9 litres for this model only. In order to keep the bonnet line low and maintain constant oil pressure at high cornering speeds, the engine was fitted with a dry sump lubrication system. The oil filler cap is mounted on the right-hand front wing, with the oil level rod attached to the filler cap rather than using a conventional dipstick. The M100 is an exceptionally smooth engine and most of the points to check on the lesser V8s also apply to it, including potential faults with the fuel-injection system and noisy timing chains. The water pump may also fail.

Diesel engines

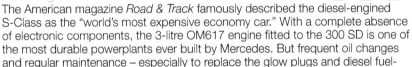

The American magazine *Road & Track* famously described the diesel-engined S-Class as the "world's most expensive economy car." With a complete absence of electronic components, the 3-litre OM617 engine fitted to the 300 SD is one of the most durable powerplants ever built by Mercedes. But frequent oil changes and regular maintenance – especially to replace the glow plugs and diesel fuel-

The first 300 SD cars sold had a rather brash 'turbo diesel' badge on the boot lid.
(Courtesy Mercedes-Benz Classic)

The five-cylinder OM617 was the first in a long line of turbocharged diesel engines.
(Courtesy Mercedes-Benz Classic)

injection pump – are essential. Look therefore for parts or workshop bills to confirm that the seller has carried out these jobs. If the engine appears to run poorly, this may be due to leaks in the vacuum lines; exceptionally, at very high mileages, the vacuum pump may fail (replacements are available). No 300 SD is going to seem fast by modern-day standards, but if the car feels dramatically slow, this may be due to failure of the Garrett turbocharger.

Exhaust system

The OEM system fitted to the different models of the W116 is generally long-lived. Replacements are no longer available from Mercedes-Benz itself, but good-quality substitutes, including stainless-steel systems, are available.

Transmission

Score only one of the following two sections (on the usual 4-3-2-1 scale) depending on whether the car you are assessing is fitted with manual or automatic transmission.

Manual transmission

Cars fitted with manual gearboxes are rare in the UK and US, but more common in continental Europe. If you

A replacement stainless-steel exhaust has been fitted to this 450 SEL 6.9.
(Courtesy Alexandre Puigvert)

Four-speed manual now rarely seen. (Courtesy Mercedes-Benz Classic)

expect to do a lot of high-speed cruising, the five-speed manual on the 280 S/SE is a desirable option, as it provides a taller top gear. The gearchange is naturally quite notchy, but the clutch is surprisingly light for such a large-engined car. There are few, if any, problems specific to the manual transmission on the W116.

Automatic transmission

The majority of all W116s were supplied with automatic transmission, which is well-suited to the car. The three-speed automatic transmission fitted to the V8

The three-speed automatic transmission in this 450 SEL 6.9 features Mercedes' traditional stepped gate. (Courtesy Artcurial Motorcars/Dirk de Jager)

petrol-engined cars has a torque converter and is intrinsically smoother than the older design of four-speed gearbox on the 280 S/SE, while the 6.9 has taller gearing for high-speed cruising on the autobahn. If well maintained, with regular fluid changes, none of the cars should suffer from jerky changes. The rear axle is tough, with only occasional whine from the diff. Vibration from the transmission may be due to cracks in the propshaft flex discs. If you detect clonks from the transmission, the propshaft joints should be examined for wear. The transmission can be rebuilt, but a full overhaul will be costly.

Suspension

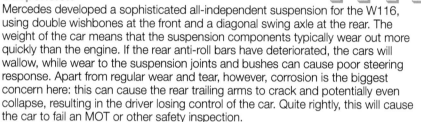

Mercedes developed a sophisticated all-independent suspension for the W116, using double wishbones at the front and a diagonal swing axle at the rear. The weight of the car means that the suspension components typically wear out more quickly than the engine. If the rear anti-roll bars have deteriorated, the cars will wallow, while wear to the suspension joints and bushes can cause poor steering response. Apart from regular wear and tear, however, corrosion is the biggest concern here: this can cause the rear trailing arms to crack and potentially even collapse, resulting in the driver losing control of the car. Quite rightly, this will cause the car to fail an MOT or other safety inspection.

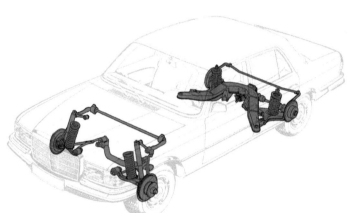

This cutaway diagram shows the key components in the W116's all-independent suspension. (Courtesy Mercedes-Benz Classic)

Hydropneumatic suspension (6.9 only – consider for Suspension score above)

For its 6.9-litre flagship, Mercedes developed a Citroën-derived self-levelling hydropneumatic suspension system, which gave a ride far superior to any other W116. On European-market cars, the ride height can be adjusted to provide additional ground clearance by means of a knob under the main instrument cluster.

If the ride feels hard, however, or if the car fails to rise properly when the engine is started, a suspension overhaul will be needed. While the system is undeniably complex, problems can certainly be dealt with by specialists. The parts specific to

One of the suspension spheres on the 6.9.
(Courtesy Alexandre Puigvert)

Large-diameter steering wheel typical
of Mercedes cars in the 1970s.
(Courtesy Bonhams)

the 6.9 are nonetheless expensive (height control valves, for example, cost ●x1440) and in some cases (such as the suspension struts and ball joints) are only available from independent suppliers, often as reconditioned items.

The most common problems include leaks from the hydraulic lines and pipes: replacing these is a major undertaking, so expect a large labour bill for the work. The suspension uses a set of spheres (or accumulators) filled with nitrogen and fluid at each corner of the car: it helps if the car is driven regularly, but they should be refilled in any event every two to three years. After ten years, however, they are likely to need replacement: over time, the rubber diaphragm inside them disintegrates, allowing the gas inside to escape. The spheres can be reconditioned by Citroën specialists or replacements obtained from Germany. They are relatively easy to change at the rear, less so at the front, due to their location.

Steering

For the W116, Mercedes retained its traditional recirculating-ball steering, which was still well thought of at the time. This should be adjusted regularly, to avoid excessive play, but this job is often skimped as it is difficult to access. The hydraulic damper fitted should also be replaced if worn.

Tyres [4] [3] [2] [1]

Does the car have a set of matching tyres from a reputable brand? Examine the tread depth across the width of the tyre and check the DOT code on the sidewall to see when they were manufactured. Rubber hardens over time, making the tyres less responsive and ultimately liable to cracking. Look too for any signs of uneven wear, suggesting that the suspension is misaligned, due either to a poorly executed repair job or previous accident damage.

You will probably need to turn to a specialist supplier of classic tyres to find the original specification tyres. The 215/70 VR14 Michelin XWX tyres exclusively fitted to the 450 SEL 6.9 are very expensive (as much as ●x465 ... per corner!).

Tyres should be checked for ageing as well as tread depth. (Courtesy Artcurial Motorcars/ Christophe Gasco)

Brakes [4] [3] [2] [1]

All models of the W116 were equipped with disc brakes all round, with ABS available from 1978 onwards. The front brake pads wear quite fast (typically lasting 10,000 miles), due to the weight of the car and, in the case of the 6.9, its high-performance. If the brakes seem slow to respond or you hear a grinding noise, the pads are probably worn. They should be replaced promptly, to avoid damage to the discs (rotors), which should be good for 30-40,000 miles. On all cars, the brake fluid should be changed regularly (at least every two years): otherwise, this will gradually absorb moisture, impairing braking performance. For later cars fitted with ABS, if the warning light stays on, it may simply be due to a dirty or faulty sensor or cable rather than anything more sinister.

Right-hand drive (RHD) cars, as sold in the UK, had a different design of parking brake, using an umbrella-type handle at the far end of the dashboard, rather than the foot pedal and pull-out knob on left-hand drive (LHD) models. Whichever type is fitted, make sure it holds the car securely.

On LHD cars, the pull-out knob next to the light switch is used to release the handbrake ... (Courtesy Bonhams)

... whereas RHD cars featured a pull-out handle at end of the dash.

Vacuum system

Like other Mercedes models from this period, the W116 used a vacuum-operated central locking system. A slight difference in the time at which each door unlocks is perfectly normal, but if they do not unlock properly, there may be a leak somewhere in the circuit, which can be difficult to locate. The vacuum pump is generally reliable. If you can, take a look at the vacuum reservoir under the front bumper: the fixings for this can corrode or break away, while the reservoir itself may begin to rot.

Underbody

With the car on a lift, look for any signs of rust on the underbody and in particular at the chassis legs near the rear wings and the subframes: in extreme cases, these can crack. A fresh or over-generous application of underseal should make you wary.

Professional inspection

Having your car inspected by a specialist can often give you extra peace of mind when buying a car. No genuine seller should object to this, provided of course that you cover any costs involved. A professional inspection in a workshop will give you the chance to look at the car on a lift and to carry out some additional checks, such as the valve clearances and cylinder compressions, which require specialist equipment.

Evaluation procedure

Add up the total points from each section.

Score: 120 (6.9) or 116 (all other models) = perfect; 90 or 87 = good; 60 or 58 = average; 30 or 29 = buyer beware! Cars scoring over 90 or 87 should be completely usable and require the minimum of repair or rectification, although continued service maintenance and care will be required to keep them in good condition. Cars scoring between 60 and 89 (6.9) or 58 and 87 (other models) will require serious work (at much the same cost regardless of score). Cars scoring between 30 and 59 (6.9) or 29 and 57 (other models) will require very careful assessment of the repair costs needed.

10 Auctions
– sold! Another way to buy your dream

Auction pros & cons

Pros: Prices are often lower than those of dealers or private sellers and you might grab a real bargain on the day. Auctioneers have generally established clear title with the seller. At the venue you can usually examine documentation relating to the vehicle.

Cons: You have to rely on a sketchy catalogue description of condition and history. The opportunity to inspect is limited and you cannot drive the car. Auction cars are often a little below par and may require some work. It's easy to overbid. There will usually be a buyer's premium to pay in addition to the auction hammer price.

Which auction?

Auctions by established auctioneers are advertised in car magazines and on the auction houses' websites. A catalogue, or a simple printed list of the lots for auctions might only be available a day or two ahead, though often lots are listed and pictured on auctioneers' websites much earlier. Contact the auction company to ask if previous auction selling prices are available, as this is useful information (details of past sales are often available on websites). Large numbers of Mercedes sell at auction, and some auction houses have, on occasion, run special single-make sales devoted to the marque.

Catalogue, entry fee, and payment details

When you purchase the catalogue of vehicles in an auction, it often acts as a ticket allowing two people to attend the viewing days and the auction. Catalogue details tend to be comparatively brief, but will include information such as 'one owner from new, low mileage, full service history,' etc. It will also usually show a guide price to give you some idea of what to expect to pay and will tell you what is charged as a 'Buyer's premium.' The catalogue will also contain details of acceptable forms of payment. At the fall of the hammer an immediate deposit is usually required, the balance payable within 24 hours. If the plan is to pay by cash, there may be a cash limit. Some auctions will accept payment by debit card. Sometimes credit or charge cards are acceptable but will often incur an extra charge. A bank draft or bank transfer will have to be arranged in advance with your own bank as well as with the auction house. No car will be released before all payments are cleared. If delays occur in payment transfers, then storage costs can accrue.

Buyer's premium

A buyer's premium will be added to the hammer price: don't forget this in your calculations. It is not usual for there to be a further state tax or local tax on the purchase price and/or on the buyer's premium.

Viewing

In some instances, it's possible to view on the day or days before, as well as in the hours prior to the auction. There are auction officials available who are willing to help out by opening engine and luggage compartments and to allow you to inspect the interior. While the officials may start the engine for you, a test drive is out of the question. Crawling under and around the car as much as you want is permitted, but you can't suggest that the car you are interested in be jacked up, or attempt to do the job yourself. You can also ask to see any documentation available.

Bidding

Before you take part in the auction, decide your maximum bid – and stick to it! It may take a while for the auctioneer to reach the lot you are interested in, so use that time to observe how other bidders behave. When it's the turn of your car, attract the auctioneer's attention and make an early bid. The auctioneer will then look to you for a reaction every time another bid is made, usually the bids will be in fixed increments until the bidding slows, when smaller increments will often be accepted before the hammer falls. If you want to withdraw from the bidding, make sure the auctioneer understands your intentions – a vigorous shake of the head when he or she looks to you for the next bid should do the trick! Assuming that you are the successful bidder, the auctioneer will note your card or paddle number, and from that moment on you will be responsible for the vehicle. If the car is unsold, either because it failed to reach the reserve or because there was little interest, it may be possible to negotiate with the owner, via the auctioneers, after the sale is over.

Successful bid

There are two more items to think about. How to get the car home, and insurance. If you can't drive the car, a trailer, your own or hired, is one way, another is to have the vehicle shipped using the facilities of a local company. The auction house will also have details of companies specialising in the transfer of cars.

Insurance for immediate cover can usually be purchased on site, but it may be more cost-effective to make arrangements with your own insurance company in advance, and then call to confirm the full details.

eBay and other online auctions

eBay and other online auctions could land you a car at a bargain price, though you'd be foolhardy to bid without examining the car first, something most vendors encourage. A useful feature of eBay is that the geographical location of the car is shown, so you can narrow your choices to those within a realistic radius of home. Be prepared to be outbid in the last few moments of the auction. Remember, your bid is binding and that it will be very, very difficult to get restitution in the case of a crooked vendor fleecing you – caveat emptor!

Be aware that some cars offered for sale in online auctions are 'ghost' cars. Don't part with any cash without being sure that the vehicle actually exists and is as described (usually pre-bidding inspection is possible).

Auctioneers

Barrett-Jackson www.barrett-jackson.com/ **Bonhams** www.bonhams.com/ **Coys** www.coys.co.uk/ **eBay** www.eBay.com/ **H&H** www.handh.co.uk/ **RM Sotheby's** www.rmsothebys.com/ **Shannons** www.shannons.com.au/ **Silver** www.silverauctions.com

11 Paperwork
– correct documentation is essential!

The paper trail
Enthusiasts' cars often come with a large portfolio of paperwork accumulated by a succession of proud owners. This documentation represents the real history of the car and shows the level of care the car has received, how it's been used, which specialists have worked on it and the dates of major repairs.

Registration documents
All countries/states have some form of registration for private vehicles, whether it's like the American 'pink slip' system or the British 'logbook' system. It is essential to check that the registration document is genuine, that it relates to the car in question, and that all the vehicle's details are correctly recorded, including chassis/VIN (Vehicle Identification Number) and engine numbers (if these are shown). If you are buying from the previous owner, his or her name and address will be recorded in the document; this will not be the case if you are buying from a dealer. In the UK, the current (Euro-aligned) registration document is named 'V5C,' and is printed in coloured sections of blue, green and pink. The blue section relates to the car specification, the green section has details of the new owner and the pink section is sent to the DVLA in the UK when the car is sold. A small section in yellow deals with selling the car within the motor trade. In April 2019 the V5C form was updated, so forms issued after this date will look slightly different.

Previous ownership records
Due to the introduction of important new legislation on data protection, it is no longer possible to acquire, from the British DVLA, a list of previous owners of a car you own, or are intending to purchase. This scenario will also apply to dealerships and other specialists, from who you may wish to make contact and acquire information on previous ownership and work carried out.

Roadworthiness certificate
Most country/state administrations require that vehicles are regularly tested to prove that they are safe to use on the public highway and do not produce excessive emissions. In the UK that test (the MOT) is carried out at approved testing stations, for a fee. In the US the requirement varies, but most states insist on an emissions test every two years as a minimum, while the police are charged with pulling over unsafe-looking vehicles.

In the UK, the test is required on an annual basis once a vehicle becomes three years old. Of particular relevance for older cars is that the certificate issued includes the mileage reading recorded at the test date and, therefore, becomes an independent record of that car's history. Ask the seller if previous certificates are available. Since 2018, cars built/first registered more than 40 years ago (which includes most W116s) are exempt from the UK MOT test, although many owners continue to have their cars inspected on a voluntary basis. If the car does still require a valid MOT certificate and this is not supplied, you should get the vehicle trailered to its new home, unless you insist that a valid MOT is part of the deal. (Not such a bad idea this, as at least you will know the car was roadworthy on the day it was tested and you don't need to wait for the old certificate to expire before having the test done.)

Road licence
The administration of nearly every country/state charges some kind of tax for the use of its road system, the actual form of the 'road licence' and, how it is displayed, varying enormously country to country and state to state.

Whatever the form of the 'road licence,' it must relate to the vehicle carrying it and must be present and valid if the car is to be driven on the public highway legally. The value of the licence will depend on the length of time it will continue to be valid. Changed legislation in the UK means that the seller of a car must surrender any existing road fund licence, and it is the responsibility of the new owner to re-tax the vehicle at the time of purchase and before the car can be driven on the road. It's therefore vital to see the Vehicle Registration Certificate (V5C) at the time of purchase, and to have access to the New Keeper Supplement (V5C/2), allowing the buyer to obtain road tax immediately.

If the car is untaxed because it has not been used for a period of time, the owner has to inform the licensing authorities, otherwise the vehicle's date-related registration number will be lost and there will be a painful amount of paperwork to get it re-registered.

Valuation certificate
A private vendor may have a recent valuation certificate, or letter signed by a recognised expert stating how much he, or she, believes the particular car to be worth (such documents, together with photos, are usually needed to get 'agreed value' insurance). Generally, such documents should act only as confirmation of your own assessment of the car rather than a guarantee of value. The easiest way to find out how to obtain a formal valuation is to contact the owners' club.

VIN and option data
Every Mercedes left the factory with a detailed data card, specifying the exact model, colour and trim, and the codes for each option fitted (eg 410 for an electric sliding roof). This information is also stamped on a metal plate at the front of the engine bay or sometimes (in North America) supplied separately. These codes – which you can look up on many online sites – should correspond to the actual equipment on the car you are viewing and provide valuable confirmation of its authenticity. If the card is missing, the Mercedes-Benz' Classic department in your

VIN plate with sequence starting 116 036 denoting a 450 SEL 6.9.

country may be able to supply a replacement. These codes are repeated on the stamped metal plate on the bonnet slam panel.

The 17-digit VIN on the data card should tally with that on the car, which you can find on a plate on the bonnet slam panel and stamped on the bulkhead at the back of the engine bay. The engine number is stamped on the cylinder block.

Service history

Try to obtain as much service history and other paperwork pertaining to the car as you can. Naturally, dealer stamps, or specialist garage receipts score most points in the value stakes. However, anything helps in the great authenticity game, items like the original bill of sale, handbook, parts invoices and repair bills adding to the story and the character of the car. Even a brochure correct to the year of the car's manufacture is a useful document and something that you could well have to search

Extensive paperwork will help confirm a car's history and authenticity.
(Courtesy Artcurial Motorcars/Dirk de Jager)

Engine performance alone is still no convincing argument in the luxury class.

Safety and comfort are just as important. It is a fact that the abilities of the Mercedes-Benz S-Class engines lie in the sports-car category. But that's to be expected and does not need to be harped on. Our goal is not to challenge drivers, but to fit automobiles to them.

The way the Mercedes-Benz S-Class reaches this goal is the blending-together of a high per-

formance power plant, a safety standard which is a model for the automobile industry, and comfort that continues for hour after hour of driving. These are the construction priorities at Daimler-Benz, and they come together with a class of workmanship that is known all over the world. The advantage, of course, is not the reputation but the result: the value of the automobile lasts

far beyond the norm. This is not simply a purchase; it's an investment.

If you are not willing to accept compromises in your choice of an automobile, get in touch with your Mercedes-Benz dealer.

Mercedes-Benz.
The way every car should be built.

A period advertisement like this is a welcome bonus.
(Courtesy Mercedes-Benz Classic)

hard to locate in future years. If the seller claims that the car has been restored, then expect receipts and other evidence from a specialist restorer.

If the seller claims to have carried out regular servicing at home, ask what work was completed and when, and seek some evidence of it being carried out. Your assessment of the car's overall condition should tell you whether the seller's claims are genuine.

Restoration photographs

If the seller tells you that the car has undergone significant work, ask to be shown a series of photographs taken while the work was underway. These should help you gauge the thoroughness of the work. If you buy the car, ask if you can have all the photographs, as they form an important part of the vehicle's history. It's surprising how many sellers are happy to part with their car and accept your cash but want to hang on to their photographs! In the latter event, you may be able to persuade the vendor to get a set of copies made.

12 What's it worth?

– let your head rule your heart

Condition

If the car you've been looking at is really bad, then you've probably not bothered to use the marking system in Chapter 9 – 60-minute evaluation. You may not have even got as far as using that chapter at all!

If you did use the marking system in Chapter 9, you'll know whether the car is in Excellent (maybe concours), Good, Average or Poor condition or, perhaps, somewhere in between these categories. Many enthusiasts' car magazines run a regular price guide. If you haven't bought the latest editions, do so now and compare their suggested values for the model you are thinking of buying; also look at the auction prices they're reporting. The values published tend to vary from one magazine to another, as do their scales of condition, so read carefully the guidance notes they provide. Bear in mind that a recent show winner could be worth more than the highest scale published. Assuming that the car you have in mind is not in show/concours condition, then relate the level of condition that you judge the car to be in with the appropriate guide price. How does the figure compare with the asking price? Before you start haggling with the seller, consider what effect any variation from standard specification might have on the car's value. If you are buying from a dealer, remember there will be a dealer's premium on the price. Finally, values of the 450 SEL 6.9 are climbing strongly, so don't wait too long!

A sliding roof is a popular extra, especially on cars without air-conditioning.
(Courtesy RM Auctions ©2018)

Desirable options/extras

Standard equipment on the W116 was surprisingly modest, especially on the first six-cylinder models sold in continental Europe, with upholstery in MB-Tex (vinyl) or patterned cloth, rather than leather or velour, for example. Power-operated

450 SEL with very rare division originally used at the UN. (Courtesy Artcurial Motorcars/ Christophe Gasco)

A large fridge is an unusual option. Courtesy Artcurial Motorcars/ Christophe Gasco)

windows, a radio and rev counter were all extras, so you shouldn't take it for granted that they will be fitted to all the cars you view.

Cars sold in North America were generally better equipped, as were the 450 SEL and 6.9 models sold in Europe, with velour or leather upholstery and all-round power-operated windows; many of these models also came with cruise control and air-conditioning or climate control.

Further desirable options include an electric sliding roof and alloy wheels. An original stereo, such as a high-end Becker Mexico, is now highly valued. Other options – typically found on top-end 450 SEL and 6.9 models – included a limousine-style division between the front and rear seats, an early in-car telephone system, and even a fridge in the luggage compartment, but these are rarely seen on cars for sale now.

Undesirable features

Cars with manual transmission are generally less sought-after than automatics. Most enthusiasts today put a premium on originality, so body kits (even from reputable firms such as AMG, Brabus or Lorinser), non-standard alloy or chrome wheels and chrome wheelarch extensions (which harbour rust, in any case) will put off many would-be buyers. So too will non-standard steering wheels and modern stereos inside the car.

Colours are always a personal matter, but dark colours such as black, grey and dark blue seem to suit the car's lines and offset its abundant chrome trim; they have probably aged better than the bold solid colours that Mercedes also offered in the 1970s, although these also have their fans.

Not all buyers will take to this car's AMG bodykit and alloy wheels.
(Courtesy Tom Wood ©2018 RM Sotheby's)

Chrome alloy wheels were more popular in the US than in Europe.
(Courtesy Robin Adams ©2015 RM Sotheby's)

Striking a deal

Negotiate on the basis of your condition assessment, mileage, and fault rectification cost. Also take into account the car's specification. Be realistic about the value, but don't be completely intractable: a small compromise on the part of the vendor or buyer will often facilitate a deal at little real cost.

13 Do you really want to restore?
– it'll take longer and cost more than you think

With relatively few examples of the W116 in excellent condition coming up for sale, you may be tempted to restore a car from scratch, or buy one that was first restored, perhaps to lower standards than today, many years ago. For some enthusiasts, nothing can match deciding exactly which parts to refurbish or replace, and carrying out or managing that work yourself. Or you may be drawn to a particular car that has been handed down from family or friends.

If you do decide to take on a restoration project, check carefully when viewing a car to see which parts come with it: the more complete it is, the better! Apart from the cost of some items, bear in mind the time you may need to track down hard to come by parts. If you go ahead, be sure to take plenty of photographs documenting the work you have done.

In nearly every case, however, buying a car to restore will be a decision made with the heart rather than the head: values of the W116 are simply too low to justify the costs involved, especially when body rather than mechanical work is required. There are two main reasons for this. First, the W116's body construction is quite elaborate, with the sills comprising inner, intermediate and outer sections, for example, while safety features such as the crumple zones add to its complexity. All this adds to the time – and hence the cost – of carrying out repairs. Secondly, as with many classic Mercedes, the body and trim parts required for a restoration can be very expensive. (See Chapter 2 – Cost considerations, for some examples.) When parts such as door cards or the rear parcel shelf are no longer available, it may be possible to make up replacements, but specialists' labour costs will soon tot up. A modestly-equipped 280 SE may cost less to refurbish than a 'fully loaded' 450 SEL, but its market value once restored will be lower, too.

Climate control and Becker stereo: nice to have but can be expensive to refurbish. (©2018 Courtesy RM Auctions)

Even for the more valuable 450 SEL 6.9, it is hard to make an economic case for a full restoration, which could cost as much as ⬤x100,000. The sophisticated features of this model quickly add to the cost of a comprehensive restoration: although the superbly effective hydropneumatic suspension can be rebuilt, parts such as the ride height control valve do not come cheap. Even routine mechanical components are often more expensive on the 6.9 than on other models. The 6.9 typically came very highly equipped, with features such as climate control, power-operated windows all round and lavish burr walnut trim: all of these will add to your pleasure in owning the car but also push up the bill for a complete restoration.

Paint faults generally occur due to lack of protection/maintenance, or to poor preparation prior to a respray or touch-up. Measuring the paint depth on each panel will help confirm if all the paint is original. Some of the following conditions may be present in the car you're looking at:

Orange peel

This appears as an uneven paint surface, similar to the skin of an orange. This fault is caused by the failure of atomised paint droplets to flow into each other when they hit the surface. It's sometimes possible to rub out the effect with proprietary paint cutting/rubbing compound or very fine grades of abrasive paper. A respray may be necessary in severe cases. Consult a bodywork repairer/paint shop for advice on the particular car.

Orange peel.

Cracking

Severe cases are likely to have been caused by too heavy an application of paint (or filler beneath the paint). Also, insufficient stirring of the paint before application can lead to the components being improperly mixed, and cracking can result. Incompatibility with the paint already on the panel can have a similar effect. To rectify the problem, it is necessary to rub down to a smooth, sound finish before respraying the problem area.

Crazing

Sometimes the paint takes on a crazed rather than a cracked

Cracking and crazing.

appearance when the problems mentioned under 'Cracking' are present. This problem can also be caused by a reaction between the underlying surface and the paint. Paint removal and respraying the problem area is usually the only solution.

Blistering

Almost always caused by corrosion of the metal beneath the paint. Usually perforation will be found in the metal and the damage will usually be worse than that suggested by the area of blistering. The metal will have to be repaired before repainting.

Micro blistering

Usually the result of an economy respray where inadequate heating has allowed moisture to settle on the car before spraying. Consult a paint specialist, but usually damaged paint will have to be removed before partial or full respraying. Can also be caused by car covers that don't 'breathe.'

Fading

Some colours, especially reds, are prone to fading if subjected to strong sunlight for

The paintwork on this 450 SEL is blistering badly next to the chrome trim.

Micro blistering.

long periods without the benefit of polish protection. Sometimes proprietary paint restorers and/or paint cutting/rubbing compounds will retrieve the situation. Often a respray is the only real solution.

Peeling

Often a problem with metallic paintwork when the sealing lacquer becomes damaged and begins to peel off. Poorly applied paint may also peel. The remedy is to strip and start again!

Dimples
Dimples in the paintwork are caused by the residue of polish (particularly silicone types) not being removed properly before respraying. Paint removal and repainting is the only solution.

Dents
Small dents are usually easily cured by the 'Dentmaster' or equivalent process, that sucks or pushes out the dent (as long as the paint surface is still intact). Companies offering dent removal services usually come to your home: consult your telephone directory or search online.

S-Class buyers in the 1970s were often bolder in their choice of paint colours than today. (Courtesy Robin Adams ©2015 RM Sotheby's)

15 Problems due to lack of use

– just like their owners, S-Class cars need exercise!

It is not uncommon to find cars offered for sale after being laid up for many years: they may have covered an attractively low mileage, but lack of use can bring its own problems.

Seized and rusted components

Pistons in callipers, slave and master cylinders can seize. The parking brake can also seize if the cables and linkages rust, particularly on cars with automatic transmission, whose owners may not use it at all, simply putting the transmission selector in 'P.'

Fluids

All filters and fluids should be replaced at regular intervals, and, if fitted, the air-conditioning recharged. Good-quality coolant is essential to avoid premature corrosion of components in the engine, cooling and heating system, and to avoid the risk of serious damage. Silt settling and solidifying can result in overheating. Brake fluid absorbs water from the atmosphere and should be renewed straightaway on any car which has been left standing.

Fuel system

If the car has not been used for a long time, the fuel tank should be drained and any rust or sediment dealt with before refilling it with fresh fuel. The fuel-injection system can play up or the injectors seize, particularly on pre-76 cars fitted with the earlier Bosch D-Jetronic system. The operation of the fuel pump should also be checked.

Tyre problems

Tyres that have had the weight of the car on them in a single position for some time will develop flat spots, resulting in some (usually temporary) vibration. The tyre walls may have cracks or (blister-type) bulges, meaning new tyres are needed. Even if the tyres appear to be in good condition, check the DOT code on the sidewall, which will show you the week and year of manufacture. As tyres age, the rubber hardens and the tyres will perform less well.

Shock absorbers (dampers)

With lack of use, the dampers will lose their elasticity or even seize. Creaking, groaning and stiff suspension are signs of this problem.

This tyre is from week 13 of 2015, as shown by the '1315' DOT code.

Rubber and plastic

Radiator hoses may have perished and split, possibly resulting in the loss of all coolant. Window and door seals can harden and leak. Gaiters and boots can crack. Wiper blades will harden. The insulation foam under the bonnet (hood) will inevitably perish.

Insulation pads are inexpensive to replace.

Interior trim

On cars with leather upholstery, the hide needs regular conditioning (every six months) if it is to stay supple. Cars left in the sun can suffer from dried or cracked dashboards. Velour or cloth trim can fade, especially in exposed areas like the top of the rear seat.

Leather upholstery needs to be fed regularly to continue looking good. (Courtesy GGE Classic)

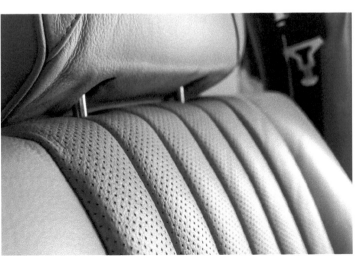

Electrics

The battery will be of little use if it has not been charged for many months. If a car is left standing for several weeks, connecting it to a trickle charger will keep it in good condition. If acid has been allowed to leak out from the battery, the metal underneath it may have rusted through.

Earthing/grounding problems are common when the connections have corroded. Wiring insulation can harden and fail. Power-operated windows can seize, particularly in the rear, where they are used less frequently. The speedometer cable can dry out, resulting in the needle fluttering.

Rotting exhaust system

Exhaust gas contains a high water content, so exhaust systems corrode very quickly from the inside when the car is not used. This even applies to stainless-steel systems.

16 The Community
– key people, organisations and companies in the W116 world

Owners of the W116 S-Class will find plenty of organisations and individuals ready to help them look after their cars.

Clubs

Mercedes-Benz Classic (www.mercedes-benz.com/en/classic/) supports more than 80 independent clubs worldwide, many of which have model registers dedicated to the W116. Benefits available to members include technical helplines and other information, discounted services (such as insurance), club magazines and the chance to join frequent social and driving events. You can find out more at:
- UK: www.mercedes-benz-club.co.uk/
- North America: www.mbca.org
- Other countries: specials.mercedes-benz-classic.com/en/club/#ger
    There is also a large online special interest group for the W116 at www.w116.org.

Specialists

In North America, it's worth starting with one of the 85 local sections of the club, which should be able to recommend a dealer or workshop near you.

In the UK, many independent Mercedes specialists such as these often sell W116s and can handle servicing and other repair work on them:
- Avantgarde Classics (Staffordshire): www.avantgardeclassics.co.uk/
- Charles Ironside (Hampshire): www.charlesironside.co.uk/
- Cheshire Classic Benz: www.ccbenz.co.uk/
- Edward Hall (Buckinghamshire): www.edward-hall.co.uk/
- John Haynes Mercedes (West Sussex): www.john-haynes.com/
    You will find listings for many other companies in the club directories and in the magazines below.

Parts and accessories

You can check (in English) which parts for the W116 remain available from Mercedes-Benz at https://teilesuche.mercedes-benz-classic.com/. For those parts no longer available, independent suppliers such as these may be able to help:
- UK – Mercedes Parts Centre: mercedes-parts-centre.co.uk/, Mercman: http://mercman.net/and PFS Parts: www.partsformercedes-benz.com/
- US – Pelican Parts: www.pelicanparts.com/Mercedes-Benz/index-SC.htm
- The German specialist Niemöller also has an English-language website at www.niemoeller.de/en.

Useful sources of information

Several English-language magazines cater to classic Mercedes enthusiasts and often feature the W116:
- *Mercedes Enthusiast* (monthly – www.mercedesenthusiast.co.uk/) and *Classic Mercedes* (quarterly - www.classicmercedesmagazine.com/) can be found at large newstands in both the UK and North America, or obtained on subscription.
- *Mercedes-Benz Classic* is published by Mercedes itself three times a year:

A US-spec W116 alongside the C 111-III record car in 1977.
(Courtesy Mercedes-Benz Classic)

subscribe at www.mercedes-benz.com/en/mercedes-benz/lifestyle/classic-magazine/subscription/
• *Mercedes Driver* is published every two months in English and is also available at large newstands or on subscription from https://shop.kelsey.co.uk/.

Bernd Koehling's book *Mercedes-Benz: Everything you want to know about the W116* (www.benz-books.com) is devoted to the W116, while James Taylor's book, *Mercedes-Benz S-Class 1972-2013* (Crowood Press), tells the story of the W116 and the generations of S-Class that followed. Although Brooklands Books' collection of period road tests of the W116 is no longer in print, used copies do come up for sale; the UK owners' club and the w116.org website (see above) have also archived a number of road test articles.

For enthusiasts who want to carry out repair work themselves, Haynes covers the 350 and 450 SE/SEL models of the W116 in its series of Workshop Manuals. Kent Bergsma's informative Mercedes Source channel on YouTube features more than 150 'how-to' videos on the W116. In the UK, the official club (https://mercedes-benz-club.co.uk/) has archived a large number of helpful articles from its magazine, covering common problems and how to repair them. Even if you do not plan on doing the work yourself, these resources provide valuable guidance on how difficult (and potentially expensive) a job may be.

17 Vital statistics
– essential data at your fingertips

Production figures

Model	Production period	Number of units
280 S	1972-1980	122,848
280 SE	1972-1980	150,593
280 SEL	1973-1980	7032
Total: six-cylinder petrol models		280,473
350 SE	1972-1980	51,100
350 SEL	1973-1980	4266
450 SE	1972-1980	41,604
450 SEL	1972-1980	59,578
450 SEL 6.9	1975-1980	7380
Total: V8 petrol models		163,928
300 SD	1977-1980	28,634
Grand total		473,035

Technical specifications

Model	Engine capacity (cc)	Engine type	Configuration	Peak power (bhp) at rpm	Maximum torque (lb/ft) at rpm	Transmissions available
280 S	2746	M110	Six-cylinder in-line	160/5500	166/4000	4M/5M or 4A
280 SE/SEL	2746	M110	Six-cylinder in-line	185/6000	176/4500	4M/5M or 4A
350 SE/SEL	3499	M116	V8	200/5800	232/4000	4M or 3A
450 SE/SEL	4520	M117	V8	225/5000	279/3000	3A
450 SEL 6.9	6834	M100	V8	286/4250	405/3000	3A

300 SD (turbo diesel)	2998	OM617	Five-cylinder in-line	115/ 4200	168/2400	4A

Note: power and torque figures for petrol-engined models are for European-specification cars and changed slightly during the cars' production life.

Running gear
• Independent suspension all round, with multi-link rear suspension, front and rear anti-roll bars, anti-dive and anti-squat geometry. Hydropneumatic self-levelling suspension standard on 450 SEL 6.9.
• Steering by recirculating ball, with power assistance standard on all models.
• Four-wheel disc brakes, with ABS optional from 1978. 14in wheels on all models.

The final W116, a 300 SD, coming off the production line in September 1980. (Courtesy *Mercedes-Benz Classic*)

Performance figures: selected models

Model	Top speed	0-60mph (96km/h) in seconds	Average fuel consumption (mpg: US/Imp)
280 SE manual	120mph/193km/h	9.7	13.9/16.7
450 SEL automatic	134mph/216km/h	9.1	12.2/14.7
450 SEL 6.9 automatic	140mph/225km/h	7.3	11.3/13.6
300 SD automatic	102mph/165km/h	15.0	24.0/28.8

Sources: *Autocar* (petrol-engined models) and *Road & Track* (300 SD).

Dimensions

Model	Standard-wheelbase (European spec)	Long-wheelbase (European spec)	300 SD (US-spec)
Length	195.3in/4960mm	199.2in/5060mm	205.5in/5220mm
Width	73.4-73.6in/ 1865-1870mm	73.4-73.6in/ 1865-1870mm	73.6in/1870mm
Height	56.1-56.3in/ 1425-1430mm	56.1-56.3in/ 1425-1430mm	56.1in/1425mm
Wheelbase	112.8in/2865mm	116.7in/2965mm	112.8in/2865mm
Fuel tank capacity	25.4US gal/96l	25.4US gal/96l	21.7US gal/82l
Unladen weight	3549-3814lb/ 1610-1730kg	3627-4266lb/ 1645-1935kg	3847lb/1745kg
Tyre size	280 S/SE/SEL: 185 HR 14 350 & 450 SE/SEL: 205/70 VR 14 450 SEL 6.9: 215/70 VR 14		185HR 14

Note: weight varies considerably by model, depending on equipment fitted. US models are typically five per cent heavier than equivalent European vehicles.

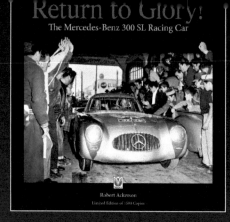

Return to Glory!
The Mercedes-Benz 300 SL Racing Car

Robert Ackerson
Limited Edition of 1500 Copies

This book chronicles the development and racing career of the 1952 Mercedes-Benz 300 SL: a car regarded as the ultimate example of the purebred sports car of the 20th century and the epitome of functional beauty and extraordinary performance. Taking second place at its 1952 Mille Miglia debut, it went on to win every one of its races that season. Dramatic photos, vivid descriptions, and dramatic recollections from the drivers ensures this book will be a joy to read and enjoy for years to come.

ISBN: 978-1-845846-17-6
Hardback • 25x25cm • 144 pages • 126 colour and b&w pictures

Explores the Mercedes-Benz W 196 R's historic roots, development, and races. The book also covers its triumphs, struggles and disappointments, as well as the spirited challenges from Maserati, Ferrari, Gordini and Lancia. Accompanying the text are hundreds of photos sourced from the legendary Daimler Archives.

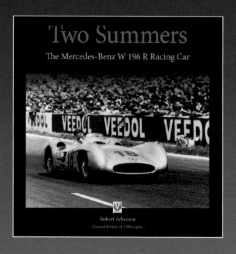

Two Summers
The Mercedes-Benz W 196 R Racing Car

Robert Ackerson
~ Limited Edition of 1500 copies ~

ISBN: 978-1-845847-51-7
Hardback • 25x25cm • 192 pages • 171 colour and b&w pictures

For more information and price details, visit our website at www.veloce.co.uk •
email: info@veloce.co.uk • Tel: +44(0)1305 260068

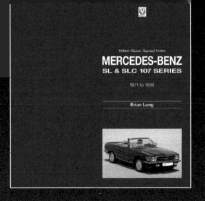

Available again after a long absence! This detailed and beautifully illustrated book covers the Mercedes-Benz 107 series, from 1971 to 1989. Written by a highly regarded motoring historian, this is THE definitive study of the subject. All major world markets are looked at, along with competition history.

ISBN: 978-1-787111-30-1
Hardback • 24.6x24.6cm • 208 pages • 355 colour and b&w pictures

The definitive history of the entire Mercedes-Benz W123 series. From the saloons/sedans, coupés, and estates/wagons, to LWB and chassis only vehicles, this book contains an overview of all the models sold in each of the world's major markets. Packed full of information and contemporary illustrations sourced from the factory.

ISBN: 978-1-845847-92-0
Hardback • 25x25cm • 192 pages • 321 colour pictures

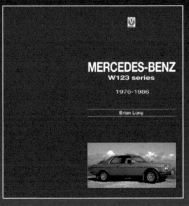

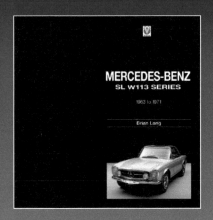

This detailed book covers the Mercedes-Benz W113 series, which ran from 1963 to 1971. Written by a highly regarded motoring writer, with many years' ownership of the Mercedes SL and SLC behind him, this is the definitive study of the subject. All models and major world markets, along with competition history, are covered. Appendices cover engine specifications, chassis numbers and build numbers.

ISBN: 978-1-845843-04-5
Hardback • 25x25cm • 208 pages • 286 colour and b&w pictures

For more information and price details, visit our website at www.veloce.co.uk • email: info@veloce.co.uk • Tel: +44(0)1305 260068

Index